CONTEN

Jürgen Klopp - I'm So Glad...

When Jürgen Klopp arrived at Anfield in October 2015, he declared himself 'the normal one' and vowed to turn Liverpool supporters from doubters to believers.

His eight-and-a-half year reign has been far from normal, leading the Reds to seven major trophies during his spell in the hotseat and he will bid farewell this summer having written himself into club folklore. He is far too humble to acknowledge it, but in years to come his name will sit alongside such LFC managerial masterminds as Bill Shankly, Bob Paisley and Sir Kenny Dalglish.

This official souvenir special magazine, the fifth in the club's ICONS series, takes us on a journey from that first memorable press conference to the current day and Klopp's Liverpool 2.0.

It takes a look at how the manager, deploying a front-footed, high pressing brand of exhilarating attacking football, led the club to Champions League glory, ended the long, long wait for a Premier League triumph, became the first LFC boss to land the FIFA Club World Cup and added a European Super Cup, an FA Cup and two League Cups to the cabinet for good measure.

Featuring historic imagery and fascinating archive interviews with the Reds' matchday programme and official club magazine, facts, stats and analysis, this souvenir helps capture the charisma behind the man who turned every Kopite around the globe into a fully-fledged believer. So sit back and enjoy the remarkable story of Liverpool FC's last eight-and-a-half years.

As the song goes, "I'm so glad that Jürgen is a Red; I'm so glad he delivered what he said."

 @lfc @liverpoolfc liverpoolfc @liverpoolfc  @liverpoolfc

Editor William Hughes **Writer** Chris McLoughlin **Production Editor** Michael McGuinness **Art Editor & Cover Design** Colin Sumpter **Design** Reach Sport design team **Contributors** Dave Ball, Ged Rea **Marketing & Communications Manager** Claire Brown **Photography** Alamy, Mirrorpix, Liverpool Echo, John Powell, Andrew Powell, Nicholas Taylor, Nikki Dyer
© Liverpool Football Club & Athletic Grounds Ltd **Published by** Reach Sport **Website** www.reachsportshop.com
Printed by Buxton Press

MADE FOR US

Why the counter-pressing, excitement-bringing, hug-giving, fist-pumping, trophy-lifting Jürgen Klopp was made for Liverpool FC…

Words: Chris McLoughlin

You take it for granted now. It's become part of Liverpool matchdays, home and away. Yet before Jürgen Klopp took charge at Anfield it was something you never saw unless the Reds won a trophy or it was the end of the season.

The Liverpool manager walk out onto the pitch to dish out hugs and handshakes at full-time, that is, then applaud supporters, irrespective of what has just happened in the 90+ minutes that went before.

Klopp's three fist-pumps to the Kop, or in front of the travelling Kop, when the Reds have enjoyed a good win are iconic. A Klopp trademark. A shared, heartfelt and passionate celebration. Sometimes of joy, sometimes of relief. Sometimes of both, but always after trying to sell the camera operator tracking him a dummy or feint that Luis Diaz would be proud of.

But it's not just about the winning. Whether Liverpool win, lose or draw, Klopp has always been a visible presence. A true responsibility-taking and thankful figurehead. And not just post-match. Take any Anfield match, for instance.

Long before kick-off, after the contractually-obliged pre-match TV interviews are completed, he waits in the Anfield tunnel for his players. The goalies go out early. They always have done, Liverpool's goalkeepers, to catch a few crosses and warm up for some shot-stopping. But when the outfield players emerge from the dressing-room the manager is ready to walk beneath the This Is Anfield sign with them. He doesn't need to. He certainly doesn't go out early for the weather. He's there for his team.

Led by Virgil van Dijk, the players head down the tunnel with the superstitious Mo Salah always last and Klopp, Pep Lijnders and Peter Krawietz right behind them. It all adds to the feeling of collective responsibility. Of being a team. Of showing up together, through the wind and rain. It's something he has done differently to his Anfield predecessors.

Liverpool's most successful manager, Bob Paisley, would be in his Anfield office half-an-hour before kick-off, watching the racing in his cardigan and slippers.

Bill Shankly would be making himself a visible presence in a different way. As soon as the visiting team arrived at Anfield he'd stand in the tunnel to cast an eye over the opposition and the mind games would begin.

"I would always keep a few bombs for Saturday," Shankly told the Liverpool Echo in his final interview before passing away in 1981. "I might say to the old guy on the Anfield door: 'Here's a box of toilet rolls. Hand them to the opposition when they come through the door'. Often I'd say it just as our opponents were walking in."

Times have changed. Away teams weren't used to the intimidating noise and power of the Spion Kop in the 1960s whereas everyone is aware of how Anfield can jangle nerves and scramble minds now, even if they can't do anything about it.

Thus visiting players aren't greeted on arrival by the Liverpool manager clutching a box of Andrex or making loud quips about their physical condition, another Shankly ploy. But they do go through their pre-match warm-ups under Jürgen's gaze.

He stands close to the halfway line in his trademark

LFC baseball cap, hands in the pockets of his Nike strike down jacket, clocking their every move. Footballers are used to people watching them, but Klopp has an aura about him. A presence. And while he has explained why he does it - "I just want to see and understand, sometimes you see a player limping a little bit, you see a player do this or that...I just try to understand what they are doing," - it can get into the heads of opponents.

"He just stares at you," Everton defender James Tarkowski told Ben Foster's 'The Fozcast'. "I always warm up right near the halfway line and I can always see him and I'm thinking I better make sure this pass is right or he's going to walk into the dressing-room and say 'that Tarkowski is having one in the warm-up, go and play on him!' I'm

"KLOPP'S THREE FIST-PUMPS TO THE KOP, OR IN FRONT OF THE TRAVELLING KOP, WHEN THE REDS HAVE ENJOYED A GOOD WIN ARE ICONIC. A KLOPP TRADEMARK. A SHARED, HEARTFELT AND PASSIONATE CELEBRATION"

> "This is a place for big football moments."
>
> Jürgen Klopp

always making sure every pass is crisp and I'm not giving it away!"

In truth, the psychological boost of seeing the Liverpool manager on the pitch pre-match, patrolling the touchline during it and applauding - or fist-pumping - the Anfield crowd afterwards is the true benefit. He leads through visibility.

Anfield has been the backbone of everything that the Reds have achieved under Klopp because he created a collective mindset of it being a fortress. But it didn't just happen overnight.

Telling Liverpool supporters that they should turn from 'doubter to believer' in his first interview with LFCTV in 2015 was the start of Klopp building all that followed, but in football actions speak louder than words. For that to happen there had to be collective belief and trust between the holy trinity of manager, players and supporters. Which is what Shankly built in the '60s as he began shaping LFC into the club it became. Into the club it still is.

"If a manager is honest and he has this natural enthusiasm, I think whilst he can't go on the field with the players he can convey it to the players, you understand?" said Shankly. "He's with them and they're with him - and they'll be successful."

Yet Shankly had also realised very early in his time as Liverpool manager that getting the Anfield crowd onboard was as important as his players believing in him. "I'm just one of the people who stands on the Kop," he said. "They think the same as I do, and I think the same as they do. It's a kind of marriage of people who like each other."

While switching to an all-Red kit to make the players look taller and having the This Is Anfield sign installed to "remind our lads who they're playing for and to remind the opposition who they're playing against," were huge psychological wins, neither would have worked had Liverpool supporters not truly believed in Shankly.

Klopp also realised that Anfield's true aura lies in its atmosphere and two games in 2015, soon after his appointment, proved crucial in building the relationship between himself and Liverpool supporters. Both were games that the Reds failed to win.

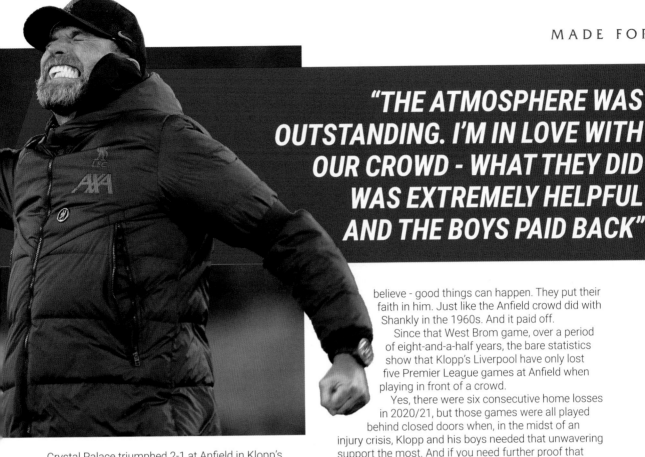

"THE ATMOSPHERE WAS OUTSTANDING. I'M IN LOVE WITH OUR CROWD - WHAT THEY DID WAS EXTREMELY HELPFUL AND THE BOYS PAID BACK"

Crystal Palace triumphed 2-1 at Anfield in Klopp's fourth home game in charge. When Scott Dann put the Eagles ahead in the 82nd minute a significant number of fans left the stadium early.

"After the goal on 82 minutes, with 12 minutes to go, I saw many people leaving the stadium," said Klopp. "I felt pretty alone at this moment. We decide when it is over. Between 82 and 94 [minutes] you can make eight goals if you like."

A month later, Liverpool were again trailing at Anfield, 2-1 to Tony Pulis's West Bromwich Albion when Baggies midfielder Craig Gardner thundered into a challenge having already put Dejan Lovren out of the game with a tackle that left the Croatian on a stretcher.

Klopp was at his most animated on the touchline and, seeing their manager at his passionate best and their players on the end of some rough treatment, the Anfield crowd responded. This time there was no mass exodus. Anfield got behind the team and in the 96th minute came the reward when Divock Origi's long-range shot took a deflection and flew in. Sometimes you make your own luck.

That 2-2 draw took the Reds up to ninth in the Premier League table. Miles from where Kopites wanted their team to be. But at full-time, Klopp took his players down to the Kop. He instructed them to hold hands and raise their arms aloft three times.

It was the kind of scene common in the Bundesliga, but never before seen at Anfield. And certainly not after scraping a 2-2 draw against West Brom. Yet the Anfield crowd bought into it. They cheered. They sang 'Li-ver-pool, Li-ver-pool'. They believed.

"I know it's only one point, but it felt like three," said Jürgen afterwards. "This moment was an explosion, it's the best I've felt since I've been here. Sometimes a point deserved in the right way is more important: for development, the style of play against a team like this. To stay in the game, that is a big moment in football. I really enjoyed this game, I enjoyed the atmosphere with my whole body."

They all laughed at us, they all mocked us, they all said our days are numbered, but they didn't understand that a seed had been planted. Kopites realised that if you stick with Klopp's Liverpool - that if you support and

believe - good things can happen. They put their faith in him. Just like the Anfield crowd did with Shankly in the 1960s. And it paid off.

Since that West Brom game, over a period of eight-and-a-half years, the bare statistics show that Klopp's Liverpool have only lost five Premier League games at Anfield when playing in front of a crowd.

Yes, there were six consecutive home losses in 2020/21, but those games were all played behind closed doors when, in the midst of an injury crisis, Klopp and his boys needed that unwavering support the most. And if you need further proof that Klopp's Anfield is the rock his empire was built upon, the fact that Crystal Palace's 1-0 win in L4 in April 2024 was only Liverpool's second home reverse in the Premier League since supporters returned to football stadiums after the pandemic dots the i and crosses the t in fortress Anfield.

"In the stadium, when they support the team, it's perfect, it's lovely," said Manchester City boss Pep Guardiola in 2019. "That's why we're involved in this business, to be involved in this kind of experience, in these stadiums. They're an exceptional team and the stadium makes an influence.

"The history speaks for itself, it's something special, but I think it's more for the quality of the team and what they do, the quality of the players and the manager they have. I would say, right now, it's the toughest stadium in Europe to go to."

Guardiola went on to describe Anfield as a 'tsunami' following a 1-1 draw in 2024, adding: "Playing here at Anfield is completely different. The environment is a reality and the players know it."

Liverpool have surfed waves of emotion and thrived off momentum under Klopp, particularly on home turf. They've been capable of scoring goals in quick succession, capable of overturning deficits to win, capable of scoring so many late goals that they set new records. And the manager is absolutely in his element in the midst of it.

After a 2-0 win against Everton in 2023, when the Anfield crowd willed their players on against a Blues side intent on slowing the game down at every opportunity, Klopp even used the 'l' word.

"The atmosphere was outstanding. I'm in love with our crowd - what they did tonight was extremely helpful and the boys paid back. Whatever the crowd would have asked for tonight I would have done it - apart from getting rid of my clothes, we don't want to torture them!"

Just like Scousers and the city of Liverpool, Klopp wears his heart on his sleeve. You can't kid a kidder, as they say around here, and seeing a manager whose emotions are real, who genuinely cares, who lives every kick like a lifelong Kopite and who somehow seems to always find the right things to say at the right time in

"IT'S RIDICULOUS, REALLY. TO WIN 26 OF YOUR OPENING 27 PREMIER LEAGUE GAMES AND DRAW THE OTHER ONE"

his second language have all endeared Jürgen to the people. But so did the football his teams have played and the success it has brought.

A sixth European Cup. A 19th league title. Who wouldn't have taken that by the end of his first four-and-a-half seasons had you been offered it when he walked through the Anfield door? But there's more.

An eighth FA Cup. A ninth and tenth League Cup. A first FIFA Club World Cup. A fourth UEFA Super Cup. A sixteenth FA Community Shield. And some of the most memorable footballing moments, matches and nights of your life.

Where do you start? The 4-1 at Man City. The 5-4 at Norwich. The Borussia Dortmund comeback. Counter-pressing. Heavy metal football. Two cup finals. Klopp was just getting started.

Sadio Mane's debut goal at Arsenal, his Merry Christmas Everton winner, his quick-fire double against Spurs. Bobby Firmino's belter at Stoke. Emre Can's acrobatics at Watford. Champions League football back on the schedule. Now we're getting warmed up.

Mo Salah. 44 goals in one season, loads of them worldies. Virgil van Dijk announcing himself in the Merseyside derby. The 4-3 against Man City. Liverpool flying forward on counter-attacks like the Red Arrows. Big Champions League nights against City and Roma. Shevchenko Park. Kyiv hurt, but Klopp had us back in business. And then he brought in Fabinho and Alisson Becker.

We went to PSG and Napoli, Belgrade and Germany. When we went the Allianz, Liverpool scored three. Porto, Barcelona, who yer tryna kid? We're the mighty Liverpool, we won it in Madrid. We won it in Madrid.

The scenes in Madrid's Plaza de Felipe II will live forever. So will the open-top bus celebrations in Liverpool. And both were made possible by the Barcelona game. Origi. Gini Wijnaldum (2). Corner taken quickly...Origi! Anfield's greatest of the great nights. Definitely under Klopp. Perhaps of all.

There could have been a Premier League title, too. Firmino's hat-trick v Arsenal. Xherdan Shaqiri's double against Man United. Salah's stunner at home to Chelsea. Origi's late winner at Newcastle. 97 points. Incredible, but agonisingly not enough. But the momentum wasn't stopping for summer.

It's ridiculous, really. To win 26 of your opening 27 Premier League games and draw the other. To take 79 out of a possible 81 points after a run of 18 successive top-flight wins. To beat all of the other 19 clubs by the end of January. To go 22 points clear by the end of February. To need six points from the final nine games to be champions. To have to wait three months to play again due to a global pandemic. To win the Premier League with seven games in hand. 99 points. From Covid-19 to Title-19. Ridiculous and ridiculously good.

Klopp ended Liverpool's 30-year wait to be champions. Had he not achieved anything else that would have still etched his name into LFC folklore. So to end the drought in such emphatic, authoritative style while his team played some exhilarating, exciting, engrossing football - combined with the steely will-to-win of mentality monsters - was something special.

Firmino's drag-back assist against Newcastle. Mane's late winner at Aston Villa. Fabinho's shot and Andy Robertson's cross for Salah at home to Man City. Thrashing Everton 5-2. Trent Alexander-Arnold's performance and goal at Leicester. The 'and now yer gonna believe us' moment after Mo saw off Man United. James Milner's clearance against Bournemouth. Beating Palace 4-0. The celebrations the following night when Man City lost at Chelsea. Naby Keita, Trent, Bobby and Alex Oxlade-Chamberlain scoring belters on coronation night at Anfield.

What a season. What a team. What a manager. What a way to end the wait. And they also picked up silverware in Istanbul and Doha along the way.

Yes, it was regrettable that Jordan Henderson lifted the Premier League trophy on an empty Kop. Yes, it hurt that Klopp and his team couldn't enjoy the most long-awaited bus parade of all. But yes, that title is in the record books. On The Champions Wall. Engraved in history.

Jürgen said to me, you know, we'll win the Premier League, you know, he said so. And even if his disciples weren't allowed through the turnstiles to celebrate he still brought the holy grail home to Anfield. His team will be remembered as one of Liverpool's greatest. So will he.

Even the spirit-sapping 'covid season' that followed had its moments. The emergence of Diogo Jota. Hitting seven at Crystal Palace and three at Arsenal. Securing Champions League football against the odds thanks to Trent's Villa winner, four goals at Old Trafford and the still-surreal moment Alisson leapt like a salmon to head home a winner at The Hawthorns. Shout out to Nat Phillips and Rhys Williams, too. The Reds also departed Melwood for the AXA Training Centre.

Klopp's journey hunters had a crack at all four pots the season after. The Beatles-inspired I Feel Fine tribute to him became the song of the season. The sound and sight of the travelling Kop performing Allez Allez Allez as Manchester City were beaten in the FA Cup semi-final at Wembley thanks to Ibou Konate and Mane gets the goosebumps going every time you recall it.

Beating Man United 5-0 at Old Trafford and 4-0 at Anfield was a 9-0 aggregate for the ages. Beating Everton 4-1 at Goodison Park was equally enjoyable. Beating AC Milan and Internazionale in back-to-back visits to the San Siro was unprecedented. Bet you still remember where you were when Origi got a 94th minute winner at Wolves, too. Thiago Alcantara was a joy to behold. Luis Diaz dribbled and dazzled.

Caoimhin Kelleher and Kostas Tsimikas emerged as penalty shoot-out heroes as Chelsea were beaten on spot-kicks in the Carabao Cup and FA Cup finals. The quadruple, never previously achieved, was still on with two games of the season to go.

It wasn't to be. Manchester City and Real Madrid - Klopp's two biggest nemeses - pipped the Reds to the Premier League and Champions League trophies by one goal each. But for Manchester City, Jürgen's Liverpool would have won much more. But for Jürgen's Liverpool, so would Manchester City.

Hitting nine against Bournemouth, seven against Manchester United and Rangers, six against Leeds and late Fabio Carvalho and Jota winners against Newcastle and Spurs provided highlights in a disappointing following campaign that had just the FA Community Shield to show for it, but Klopp was awarded the Freedom of Liverpool and in the summer of 2023 pressed the reset button. Liverpool 2.0 were born.

Darwin Nunez's double at Newcastle. Dominik Szoboszlai's stunners against Aston Villa and Leicester. Wataru Endo and Trent providing a thrilling finish against Fulham. Alexis Mac Allister's first in red in that game and his strike against Sheffield United. Nunez sending the travelling Kop wild at Nottingham Forest. And the moment of the season - Virgil van Dijk heading a Wembley winner against Chelsea as Klopp's kids won the Carabao Cup when they had school the next day.

Curtis Jones. Harvey Elliott. Stefan Bajcetic. Kaide Gordon. Conor Bradley. Jarell Quansah. Bobby Clark. James McConnell. Jayden Danns. Lewis Koumas. Trey Nyoni. Who knows where Klopp's legacy will take us?

Just like Paisley did during his last season in charge, when Liverpool won the League Cup in 1983, Klopp was asked by his skipper to lift the trophy so climbed the Wembley steps with his team. Alongside Van Dijk, arguably his greatest signing, he hoisted the silverware aloft with a beaming smile upon his face and his players next to him as thousands of believers celebrated wildly.

That is how Klopp will be remembered. As a visible presence. As a fist-pumping, hug-giving, smiling and charismatic individual. As an emotional yet astute trophy-winning manager who gave his all and gave us it all while playing entertaining football.

Liverpool was made for Jürgen Klopp and Jürgen Klopp was made for Liverpool.

2015/16

AND SO IT BEGINS

Jürgen Klopp inherited a Liverpool FC team that were 10th in the Premier League, winless after two Europa League group stage games and that had needed penalties to defeat League Two Carlisle United at Anfield in the League Cup.

So when he told LFCTV in his first interview as Reds boss that supporters must change from 'doubter to believer - now' it was going to take a huge leap of faith from Kopites, but it soon became apparent that Klopp's Liverpool could play enthralling, intense attacking football and win matches.

Away successes at Chelsea (3-1), Manchester City (4-1), Southampton (6-1 in the League Cup), Norwich City (5-4) and Aston Villa (6-0) built excitement, while Anfield was galvanised with Europa League victories against Manchester United (2-0), Borussia Dortmund (4-3) and Villarreal (3-0) that took the Reds to the final in Switzerland.

Klopp had already taken Liverpool to the League Cup final and while they returned from Wembley and Basel without silverware to show for their efforts, Liverpool supporters had already seen enough to stop doubting and start believing.

JÜRGEN KLOPP

THE FIRST INTERVIEW

On the evening that his appointment as Liverpool FC manager was officially announced, Jürgen Klopp sat down with LFCTV's Claire Rourke...

CLAIRE ROURKE: JÜRGEN, WELCOME TO LIVERPOOL FOOTBALL CLUB...
JÜRGEN KLOPP:
Thank you so much.

CR: HOW DO YOU FEEL?
JK: Great! I have no other words for this. It was a crazy day with everything that happened in Germany and all that happened here when we landed. It's an absolutely great feeling for me and a big honour to be here. It's one of the best moments in my life, I have to say. I'm here together with my family – not the whole family, one son is still at home – but we are here together and it feels like a dream.

CR: WHAT ATTRACTED YOU TO LIVERPOOL FOOTBALL CLUB?
JK: Everything. All I heard about, all I read about, all I felt when I saw, not too many matches in my life but some very important games. I love football and the intensity of football in Liverpool is very good for me. I always thought about working in England because of the kind of football and the intensity of the football, and Liverpool was first choice. Now I have got the opportunity to work here, it's the best thing I can imagine.

CR: WHAT DID YOU NEED TO CONSIDER, OR WOULD YOU SAY IT WAS AN EASY DECISION?

JK: It was not the most difficult decision. I ended my contract with Dortmund four months ago and I thought about what I would do in the future. I had to develop myself, think about all the things that had happened in the last 15 years. But then I had a holiday for four months and it was enough. It was great, but it was enough. The owners have a dream and I have a dream, and so there was not too much they had to say so I could be here... I had six very, very cool years at Dortmund and one hard year in the last one, but as a package it was perfect. But I wanted to do something new – and now I am here.

CR: LET'S TALK ABOUT ANFIELD – HOW MUCH ARE YOU LOOKING FORWARD TO THAT BECOMING YOUR HOME AND BEING THE MANAGER FOR THOSE FANS?

JK: My English is not good enough to express this! Not at the moment [anyway], you'll have to ask me this in a few months again. But of course I am pretty excited. I want to see it, I want to feel it, I want to smell it – I want to do everything. When I came here with Dortmund a year ago [for a preseason friendly] I was really excited. I came in and saw the dressing-room for the away team… For me, it was historical. It's a great place – I've been to some places in the world with football, but this was the most special place I'd been. Borussia Dortmund's stadium, Signal Iduna Park, is a great stadium and I had another perfect little, little stadium with Mainz 05, but this [Anfield] is the most historic place. I am looking forward to it and at this moment I don't know what I will feel, but it will be good.

CR: IT'LL BE PRETTY SPECIAL TO GO INTO THAT HOME-TEAM DRESSING-ROOM…

JK: Yes, of course. I hope. I'm sure!

CR: HOW IMPORTANT IS IT TO YOU TO HAVE OR CREATE THAT SPECIAL CONNECTION WITH THE SUPPORTERS?

JK: I understand football. If the people are not interested in football, we can put some sticks in the park and play football. It's still the perfect game, it's still the same game, but it's only this game because of the fans. That's what I know, what I think, what I feel. We have to entertain them, we have to make their lives better. That's what we have to do because football is not so important – we don't save lives or things like that, we are not doctors. It's our job to let them forget their problems for 90 minutes and then they can talk for three days about the last game and talk for two days about the next game.

That's how I want to live: if I am not a manager, that's the way I would live because I love this game so much. That's why I try to be as close as possible to the fans, but it's not always so possible to be close to the fans because of the job. I have to work and I need time to work, so it's not always as the fans want but it's as often as possible.

CR: BUT YOU FEEL YOU UNDERSTAND WHAT IT IS TO BE A FAN?

JK: I always understand. Maybe on Friday I can go to all the places in the stadium and someone will tell me: 'That happened here and that happened there… Stevie G shot from here, Robbie Fowler or whoever'. That's pretty cool.

CR: YOU CAN GO WHEREVER YOU WANT NOW – YOU'RE THE MANAGER OF LIVERPOOL FOOTBALL CLUB!

JK: Yeah, that's the best thing! But not during the 90 minutes. That will be the most difficult thing for me, the two benches being so close. It's so different to Germany – you could accidently hit the other coach or manager. I get a little bit emotional during a game!

CR: DO YOU THINK YOU'LL NEED TO ADAPT TO ENGLISH FOOTBALL? HOW DO YOU THINK YOU WILL ADAPT?

JK: Of course I will adapt, maybe I have to, I don't know! But in this moment I don't think about this because it's football and I know English football. I watched so many games and we played against English teams. Some things are different but that's not too important in this moment because it's only football. Don't forget, it's a game and we all have the same rules, the pitches are similar in size, so it's not so difficult.

My experience is: listen, see, feel, and then think about what you change. Now I have to do these three things and then think about what I have to change or I have

to adapt or whatever. I've [been in] football for a long time. I was a player, now I'm a manager. I don't want to make it too complicated.

CR: WHAT SIMILAR CHALLENGES DO YOU THINK YOU'LL FACE HERE AT LIVERPOOL THAT YOU FACED AT DORTMUND?

JK: Maybe this is the biggest challenge in this moment in world football [laughs], but I was never a guy for the easy way… I know what I want, but I don't want to tell it to you. First I have to talk to the players, of course. We have to find a common way. We will find a common way and who wants to do what I sometimes propose! [They] can be a good friend of mine [laughs] and it's not such a bad thing to be a good friend of mine because I am really loyal.

CR: HOW DO YOU ASSESS THE SQUAD THAT YOU'RE INHERITING HERE AT LIVERPOOL?

JK: It's good, it's good. I'm here because I believe in the potential of the team. If Liverpool ask me and I see the team and think, 'Oh my God', no, no, no. In this moment, we are not the best team in the world. Who cares? Who wants to be the best team in the world today? We want to be the best team tomorrow or another day. That's all. What I saw from outside is absolutely okay. I saw some good matches and some not so good, but it's normal in football you have some problems. You have to solve them.

The important thing is we have speed, we have technical skills, we have tactical skills, we have good defenders, good midfielders, good strikers, wingers. Now we have to see who is fit for the first game against Tottenham and then we have to make a team for this game. Then we can start. I'm not a dream man, I don't want to have Cristiano [Ronaldo] or Lionel [Messi] and all these players in one team. I want these guys [the current squad]. It was a decision for these guys. Now we start working.

CR: CAN YOU TELL US WHAT STYLE OF PLAY WE CAN EXPECT?

JK: A wild one [laughs]. In football, all the world-class teams play possession football, that's cool. I like to watch this. Bayern Munich, great team, great club; Barcelona, yes; Real Madrid; maybe on some days, Manchester City. But nobody starts as a ball-possession team. You cannot start and say: 'Okay, we have the ball and the other players have to wait'. The first thing, always, maybe in life, you need to have a stable defence. That's the first thing, always. Because you can only stay confident in a game when you know not each offensive move of the other team is a goal. That's the first thing and when you start a development nobody starts a development from the top of the table, only a few teams. You always have a little bit [of a] lower position and our position is absolutely okay...

The kind of football [I coach] is emotional. I like this, I like the emotion in the game. I like the speed in the game. You have to be a real man or woman in the game. It's hard, all things are like this. If I talk about aggressiveness, I only talk about aggressiveness against myself. I have to be harder, feel no pain or something like this, and not aggressive against the opponent because I'm not interested in fouls or things like this. I will see what is possible with this team and then we will decide how we start and when we start we'll know more...

If it's possible, can we be the hardest team to beat in the world? Let's try to be this. If you are this, it's not that far away to be a team who can win games. First of all we have to talk with all LFC fans, talk about what are expectations. Because expectations can be a real big problem: it's like a backpack of 20 kilos, it's not so cool to run with this! We have to talk about this, we have to think about this, and then we can start.

CR: DO YOU THINK YOU NEED A LOT OF TIME TO

IMPLEMENT YOUR STYLE AND PHILOSOPHY?

JK: Of course it needs a lot of time for the end, but not to start. I'm not here to promise you will see against Tottenham the absolute new LFC – but some of the new LFC would be cool. That's what we'll try to do. Everything in life takes time. To be an adult takes time. To become a football player takes time. Everything takes time. The only thing nobody gives time is development.

CR: THERE HAS BEEN A LOT OF MEDIA TALK ABOUT THE TRANSFER STRUCTURE WITHIN THIS FOOTBALL CLUB. WHAT IS YOUR TAKE ON IT AND WHAT CONVERSATIONS, IF ANY, HAVE YOU HAD WITH THE OWNERS ABOUT THAT?

JK: It's a really funny thing. It was absolutely no problem between FSG and myself. We talked about this. It's nothing. If two smart, intelligent, clever guys sit together on a table and you both want the same, where can be the problem? We all want to be successful. The only thing for me is to have the first and last word. I don't want to spend money the club doesn't have. I don't want to hold a player that doesn't want to stay. I have to work all day with these guys. Nobody will sell a player I want to work with, even if it's a good deal. Nobody wants to transfer a player without my 'yes'. So everything is okay, I don't need more.

CR: WILL YOU BE BRINGING ANY BACKROOM STAFF?

JK: Of course. My two 'brothers-in-mind', Zeljko [Buvac] and Peter [Krawietz], great guys. You will feel it when you see them. They are cool, they are football maniacs. They work pretty hard and they are my perfect partners in this job, because as a manager you always have to make decisions and always have to think about so many different things. In my opinion, it's very important that you have somebody you can talk to. We can talk about everything. I make the decisions, of course, but I need very good people around me.

CR: WHAT ARE YOU HOPING TO ACHIEVE SHORT AND LONG-TERM?

JK: Success. It's important what we can do together to change our situation. At the moment, all of the LFC family is a little bit too nervous, a little bit too pessimistic, too often in doubt. They all celebrate the game, it's a great atmosphere in the stadium, but they don't believe at the moment. They only want to see five years ago, 10 years ago, 20 years ago. History is great but it's only to remember. No, we have the possibility to write a new story if we want. For that, we have to clear a few things.

CR: FINALLY, WHAT IS YOUR MESSAGE TO THE LIVERPOOL SUPPORTERS?

JK: We have to change from doubter to believer. Now.

TWEETS OF THE MONTH

KLOPP SPECIAL

JÜRGEN KLOPP

Kop Magazine
@TheKopMagazine
Jürgen Klopp, rocking
the 1980s Kloppite look
there #LFC #Klopp

Jamie Carragher
@Carra23
I've just been cut off on
LFC TV for Jürgen Klopp!
He better be good!!

Kelly Cates
@KellyCates
I love days when football
makes grown adults
feel like kids.

Titi Camara
@TitiCamara22
#LFC congratulations
to Mr Klopp uniting the
club as one before a
ball has been kicked #KloppLFC

Borussia Dortmund
@BVB
We heard the news today,
oh boy! All the best at
The Kop, Jürgen Klopp!
All the best at @LFC! #klopplfc

Xabi Alonso
@XabiAlonso
Welcome to the Liverpool
family. YNWA Mr Klopp!!

John Arne Riise
@JARiiseOfficial
Just seen Jürgen Klopp first
interview as manager of
our great club @LFC.
Gave me goosebumps!! What a way to start!!

PB
@patrikberger73
I was at Dortmund and LFC
and it was a win-win situation
and Klopp will be no different!
World class manager @LFC #KloppforKop

THE ANFIELD WRAP
@TheAnfieldWrap
Klopp

Issue 40 of the club's official monthly magazine put the spotlight on Jürgen's first week at the helm from his initial press conference at Anfield to his opening fixture v Tottenham at White Hart Lane...

the first week

Whatsapp discussions, text messages, Facebook, Twitter, on the bus, on the train, in the corner shop. There was only one name being mentioned in the days that followed Liverpool's 1-1 draw at Goodison Park last month.

The buzz in the city and around the wider football world, the full house for the first official press conference, held at Anfield... John Hynes summarises the start of the new Reds manager's reign

Almost immediately after the derby Brendan Rodgers had departed and it very quickly became apparent that there was a good chance his replacement would be the impressive Jürgen Klopp.

Personally, as both fan and writer for the magazine I was sceptical that the appointment would go ahead. With so many rumours and so much speculation surrounding the game nowadays I stubbornly refuse to get excited by any potential new arrival until the deal is actually confirmed and the man in question is standing at Anfield wearing our colours. Yet it was hard not to become engulfed by the wave of excitement which grew and grew as it became more obvious that LFC's new manager would indeed be the former Borussia Dortmund boss.

By the Wednesday after the Merseyside derby it seemed almost a certainty, and the realisation that one of the most coveted coaches in the game was on his way had Kopites grinning from ear to ear. I even overheard a conversation where an optimistic fan suggested: "With this lad in charge we'll win the league this season."

Still, I was reluctant to get carried away or think about it too much.

"IT WAS SO HARD NOT TO BE ENGULFED BY THE TIDAL WAVE OF EXCITEMENT ALL AROUND"

He's really here!

19

That was impossible, though, as even a quick glance at my phone or online took me to people talking about Klopp. Apparently he'd even been spotted at an Audi dealership in Liverpool. Of course in reality it was someone who bore a passing resemblance, but it gave you an idea of the hype surrounding his imminent arrival.

On Thursday afternoon the story went into overdrive with reports from Germany saying he had signed a contract with Liverpool while, simultaneously, the sightings of him kept coming. Buying a Lotto ticket, sitting on a bus, in a hardware shop... If he was on Merseyside he was having a ridiculously busy day. Of course he had yet to arrive, but even the details of his flight from Dortmund to John Lennon Airport were being monitored online, 35,000 people tracking the progress of the private plane.

Around the same time as Klopp was in the air, word came through that 'a major club announcement' would be taking place at an Anfield press conference on Friday morning. It was actually happening: one of the most sought-after and admired managers in the game was to be our new gaffer and, just after 5pm, he was spotted leaving Liverpool Airport. Some people online speculated that he might jump on the 82C bus into town, but instead

"AROUND 35,000 PEOPLE TRACKED THE PROGRESS OF HIS PLANE ON TWITTER"

he was photographed in a Mercedes people-carrier heading for a city-centre hotel to meet club officials.

Finally, the seemingly inevitable news every Liverpool fan had been waiting for was confirmed at around 9pm: Klopp had signed a three-year contract and would be unveiled at Anfield the next morning, while reports emerging out of his homeland quoted the 48-year-old as saying: "From tomorrow I will be a Liverpool man 24/7."

Despite having two young kids of my own and regularly craving a good night's sleep, I found it difficult to nod off that night. Would Klopp have second thoughts and change his mind? He's always been unpredictable and, as numerous videos demonstrated, eccentric. That thought still lingered in my brain as we made our way to Anfield and the Centenary Stand for the official press conference on Friday morning for our first glimpse of him.

Naturally we weren't alone: the Reds Lounge was full to capacity with reporters, cameramen and

Any questions?

photographers from all over the globe having descended on L4. The room was buzzing, and this was even before Klopp had stepped inside. Seasoned journalists – supposedly neutral observers – had big smiles etched across their faces instead of the usual non-plussed expressions. And those members of the media with LFC allegiances were almost doing cartwheels with excitement.

Then, around 10am, a temporary hush descended as Klopp entered to be greeted by a wall of camera flashes. As he made his way to the long table in the head of the room he smiled and looked around before addressing the audience with a cheery "Good morning."

Initially Klopp seemed slightly taken aback by what the LFC media officer described as a "phenomenal turnout." He apologised for his English, something that was unnecessary as it was almost flawless – on the few occasions he was unsure of a word he eventually found the right one to get his point across.

His time with the media contained plenty of humour and he seemed relaxed throughout. But there were also moments when Klopp showed the ruthlessness required of a top manager, dismissing one question and declaring he would have the first and last word on transfers. It

At the Academy with Alex Inglethorpe

was clear that he also has a serious side. By the time he stood up from the table to leave, the impression he had made was huge. Everybody in the room agreed that he'd somehow lived up to the hype.

Walking away from the ground

"EVEN THE MOST SEASONED JOURNALISTS HAD BIG SMILES ON THEIR FACES"

that morning you felt energised. You felt much more positive about this season and the future ahead. It gave you a little glimpse of why the Borussia Dortmund players were so motivated and so willing to outrun and outplay opponents on the way to two Bundesliga titles and a Champions League final appearance.

If Jürgen Klopp can make such an impression in a press conference, imagine how his Liverpool players will feel when he sends them out to do battle at Anfield. I wouldn't want to be in their way.

His first post-press conference training session at Melwood

UNDERARMOUR.COM
AIA
BARCLAYS PREMIER LEAGUE
BARCLAYS
#SpiritoftheGame
Garuda Indonesia
balance

LIFE IN THE
FAST LANE

First game in charge: midday kick-off, Tottenham Hotspur away. The new manager took it all in his stride, as David Cottrell reports from behind the Liverpool dugout

What was it Jürgen Klopp said about sunshine footballers in his first press conference? "If you think about the weather, stay away." Wouldn't you know, those supposedly warmer climes down south (London being closer to the Equator and all that) are absent for his first game as Liverpool manager. Not that it's chilly or even raining as such, but it sure is overcast. White Hart Lane, a lovely old football ground, feels a bit like a budgie's cage today with a big grey tea-towel tossed over the top. Do the Liverpool fans care? Does Sturridge miss from five yards?

It's a long way to Tottenham Hotspur, a long way to go, especially from Seven Sisters tube station, along the endless High Road and past the Town Hall and turn-offs for Walthamstow and Wood Green.

We're making this timezone-straddling schlepp on account of rail services from overground stations closer to the stadium being suspended, according to my match-going mate who'll believe anything he mis-hears (more of him later). Though just inside the delineating North Circular Road, Spurs has always felt a good deal further out than local rivals Arsenal, at least to this particular writer/away fan when he lived in the Smoke.

23

JÜRGEN KLOPP

"FROM JUST BEHIND THE DUGOUT YOU REALISE HOW GOOD THESE PLAYERS REALLY ARE"

I'm going back a bit now, so bear with the misty eyes. The first time I went to White Hart Lane was by coach for the 1986 FA Cup semi-final against Southampton when Saints defender Mark Wright broke his leg and Ian Rush won it for Liverpool. The chorus of *You'll Never Walk Alone* from our end at full-time, as the players walked over to salute the travelling Kop, still gives me goose-bumps.

The first and last time I sat in the press box at White Hart Lane was a few years later, Saturday 18 January 1992; a rookie journalist on a weekly football magazine, moved-down to London and determined to tick off all the capital's grounds whether or not the Reds were in town. On this occasion Tottenham were playing a Southampton side which had a young powerhouse of a no9 called Alan Shearer playing alongside Iain Dowie (uncle of Liverpool Ladies striker Natasha) and potty-mouthing the nearside linesman. Upfront for Spurs: Paul Walsh, formerly of our own parish, and Gary Lineker.

Nine months later, for the Liverpool game I borrowed the season-ticket of a Spurs fan I worked with. She couldn't make the match for some reason, so there was me, sat among the home supporters right behind the goal (Paxton Road end in those days, I think), getting all sorts of funny looks off the locals, alone and forlorn with a face like a squeezed orange as they leapt up to cheer goals from Nayim and Neil Ruddock not long before he swapped the lily-white for all-red. Two-nil. Dismal.

The most recent time I saw the Reds play here? Sunday 16 August 2009, season-opener. Tottenham Hotspur 2 Liverpool 1. Assou-Ekotto's half-volleyed rocket, Gerrard's equaliser from the penalty spot, Bassong's demoralising winner, and Carragher and Skrtel's painful clash of heads. At least that time I was in the away end.

So, the here and now. Earlier this morning we took a train from South London into a King's Cross station and London skyline I barely recognised, not even since May 2014 when I was down for the three-all at Crystal Palace. Thanks to the Klopp factor, if they weren't already hard-to-come-by, tickets for this Tottenham match are now like gold-dust. Opposite me on the train down from Lime Street last night was a fella with his lad, desperate for a spare; as it goes he did get one, he tells me a week later back in the Twelfth Man before the Southampton game at Anfield.

I'm fortunate to be press-passed up today. My pal is picking up his ticket for the away end from another friend in The Antwerp Arms, a countrified little pub not five minutes from the full-throttle footfall of Tottenham High Road. In a few minutes, as they attempt to pass through the turnstiles it'll dawn on them that they've come with the wrong tickets: Chelsea v Liverpool in a fortnight's time, not Tottenham v Liverpool. Good job the Spurs staff are so understanding: after a few security checks they're allowed in a few minutes after kick-off.

I've left them to torment the Tottenham ticket-office. I want to get in the ground handy today, keen to witness Klopp's emergence from the tunnel before a phalanx of photographers. I'd forgotten how close to the action the press-box is at White Hart Lane (well, it has been 23 years). Wedged between the lads from the LFC website and a writer from *FourFourTwo* Stats Zone, I'm right behind the Liverpool dugout, flush with the halfway-line and so low I can make out the subtle camber of the pitch. Out comes Klopp, tracksuited and booted, off go the flashes. He shakes hands with Spurs boss Mauricio Pochettino and we're ready to go.

I'm torn between keeping an eye on the boss for the purposes of this piece, and watching the game unfold like everyone else in the ground. I'll come clean: the fan in me wins, so don't be expecting too much Kloppological insight. You've come this far you may as well stick with me till the end.

At this level, with no panoramic perspective from the stands, you realise how good these footballers are. There is no time or space to dwell on the ball, hardly a second to react let alone think. Instant control, incredible first-touch, pinball-passing. Peering over the heads of

substitutes Jordon Ibe, Joao Carlos Teixeira, Joe Allen, Jerome Sinclair and Connor Randall just in front of me, checking the urge to join in the songs from the away corner to our right, amid all the excitement this much registers: Klopp hugs the touchline for most of the match, but as soon as the opposition win a corner he sits down; as soon as the danger passes he's on his feet again pitchside, arms folded in front or hands clasped together behind his back. He applauds courage and cute play; urges his side forward with one arm outstretched when they win back the ball; spins back to the bench with a grimace and flick of the fringe when they concede or waste possession.

Whenever possible he touchline-coaches Divock Origi, who looks and listens and comes so close

with that first-half header against the bar. A little later Sakho's block on his own line brings a punch to the air. The manager is impassive when Lucas, penalised for a foul right by the two dugouts, barks at a gesticulating Pochettino, but he's playful with the Spurs boss when the ref, who blows for a push on Nathaniel Clyne, is berated by the home fans. In stoppage time when a Liverpool corner comes to nothing he screams at his players to get back – *GET BACK!*

Full-time. Boy, have these players put a shift in for the new gaffer. "Satisfied" is his verdict in the post-match press-conference inside the West Stand. "Our start was brilliant, we did well... When we had the ball we were not cool enough, we did not use our skills. We didn't see the right options but it's normal... We had our moments, after three days it's okay... We enjoyed it [our first game in charge] but we're not here to enjoy it... We are in, and now we can work."

The rest of us? Made-up, all things considered: manager's first game, striker shortage and a point away to a Tottenham team that whupped Man City 4-1 here last time round. Let's get home: here come Rubin Kazan.

"HE URGES HIS PLAYERS FORWARD, GRIMACES WHEN THEY GIVE THE BALL AWAY"

THE MANAGER

"I ask you to believe in this team"

Good evening and welcome to Anfield for our UEFA Europa League contest against Rubin Kazan.

First of all I would like to thank everyone for the extremely warm welcome you have given to me, my family and my staff who have also travelled to Liverpool to be part of this exciting new adventure. We have been overwhelmed by the support and enthusiasm and it has touched us greatly.

I must offer a special thanks to the owners FSG, particularly John, Tom and Mike. They have given me a wonderful opportunity. I believe they are really smart guys and I am excited about working with them.

Zeljko Buvac and Peter Krawietz extend their thanks also, having joined as members of the coaching team. They are two very important people to me and will be a big part of what we are looking to achieve here in Liverpool. I trust you will make them feel as welcome as I have.

There has been much to learn and much to experience in a short space of time, but so far it has been very positive. The staff at Liverpool FC are very passionate about the club and have shown a commitment to help us settle in and introduce our ideas. The players have also demonstrated they are committed to hard work and learning from our new ideas. This is very important because if we are to achieve success at Liverpool it will only be possible if we all take responsibility and we all work together.

It was pleasing to play a match at Tottenham Hotspur because it gave us an experience of our own and something we can work directly with now. We can look at what we did, good and not so good, and learn from it and look to improve it. Of course this is just one game but it is still our shared experience, so for that reason it is positive.

There has been just one disappointment since arriving and that has been the unfortunate injury situation. To lose young Joe Gomez and Danny Ings to knee injuries was very unfortunate and of course it means we will be without them for matches for some time. However, I am confident they will work hard on their recovery and come back stronger and ready to challenge.

Tonight we welcome our visitors from Russia, FC Rubin Kazan, to Anfield. I welcome their coach Valeri Chaly, his team, staff and their supporters. I wish them a safe and enjoyable visit to the city of Liverpool, but of course for 90 minutes we are opponents.

Finally, I would like to speak directly to the Liverpool supporters for not just this evening's game, but also the many matches that are to follow. This is my first time as manager of Liverpool for a game at Anfield and it is something that will be very important for me and my staff.

You have a vital role to play in what we are looking to achieve. You are a very special group of supporters and the atmosphere you create is unique. I ask that you believe in this team and believe that together we can achieve great things. We must all stay together and look to enjoy the experience of following such a great club. Football should be about joy and fun and that must be reflected throughout the entire organisation.

The team will go out and battle for you and look to represent you, the club and the city in how we approach our work: this is my commitment. Thank you again for the incredible support you continue to give.

You'll Never Walk Alone
Jürgen

There was the rare sight of the manager fully suited and booted for his opening night in front of the Kop. The official Liverpool FC monthly magazine was present for the start of something special

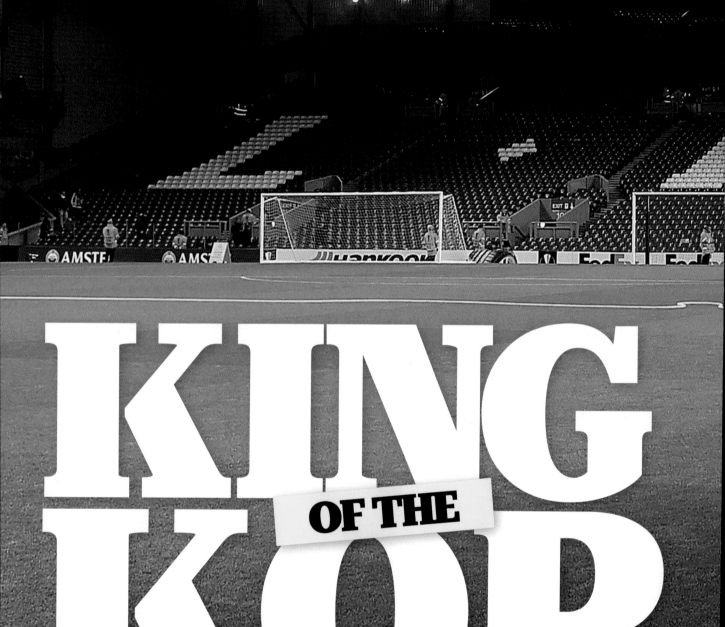

KING
OF THE
KOP

UEFA EUROPA LEAGUE

FedEx

UniCredit   enterpris   rent-a-car   enterpris

Anfield could hardly wait to welcome the boss for his first home game in charge... Chris McLoughlin keeps a close eye on Klopp as his team host Kazan

Anticipation is one of the greatest feelings you experience when following football. The excitement of what might happen – the apprehension that swirls around your mind ahead of a big game – keeps you coming back. Even if the reality doesn't always match your dreams.

Indeed, sometimes you cannot help but question your faith. Belief can ebb away. Liverpool supporters will always have hope in their hearts, but when performances and results leave you regularly frustrated enthusiasm and excitement levels dip. Jürgen Klopp sensed that when he walked through the doors at Anfield to take charge as the new manager of Liverpool Football Club. Behind the trademark thick-rimmed glasses are a fresh pair of eyes. They saw that

improving things on the pitch isn't the only task here.

Negativity can be a self-fulfilling prophecy. Expect to fail and you will. An increasingly downbeat mentality had become entrenched among Liverpool supporters. Klopp is determined to consign that to the past.

The media lapped up Klopp's 'Normal One' soundbite at his press-conference unveiling, but the line that he hoped would resonate most with Kopites came at the end of the LFC TV interview he gave to Claire Rourke the day before. Turning to the camera, looking each and every viewer in the eye, he kept it concise. "We have to change from doubter to believer. Now." The beaming smile that followed was infectious, but everyone knew the point he was making was valid.

It was evident to what extent those words had been taken on board when Liverpool took on Rubin Kazan in the Europa League at Anfield, Klopp's first home match as manager. Anfield is famous for its European nights. The reputation is earned on merit. Our eyes have seen the glory. Our songs have rang in opponents' ears. But not every European night is as atmospheric as Inter Milan 65 or St Etienne 77.

Liverpool versus Rubin Kazan in a Europa League group-stage match on a Thursday night is not Liverpool versus Chelsea in a Champions League semi-final. There's no comparison. Nor should there be. Your turkey tastes better on Christmas Day because it's a one-off and you've been looking forward to it for weeks. Even Facebook foodies don't upload their beans-on-toast photos every other Thursday night.

But this was a unique situation. Liverpudlians had a new manager to welcome and, after listening to his words and seeing our players work harder than ever in his first game at Tottenham, added effort was put in by match-going Reds. Several new banners appeared on the Kop, some of which had been given a first outing at White Hart Lane. *Jürgen's Reds: Scouse nicht Englisch* stated one.

A Bundesflagge und Handelsflagge (the German flag) had *Jürgen: Meine Held, Meine Kumpel* (Jürgen: my hero, my pal) printed upon it. *Jürgen Klopp: Kop Idol* featured on another.

Two of the most striking banners featured silhouetted images of Klopp's trademark hat and

"KLOPP HAS CHARISMA, HE CAN GALVANISE A CROWD AND HE'S VERY VISIBLE"

spectacles. *Far From Normal* read one, but the other will have struck a chord with the Liverpool boss: *Then I saw his face*, it read, *Now I'm a believer*. How apt.

The next line of that 1966 hit just happens to be 'not a trace of doubt in my mind'. We're more used to lyrics from The Beatles than The Monkees on Kop banners, but when you're changing from doubter to believer you'll take your inspiration from anywhere.

Seeing the man himself dressed in a smart club suit stride out onto the Anfield pitch during the warm-up also gave those inside Anfield an immediate lift. The ground wasn't even half-full at that point, but the proverbial glasses of those applauding were.

Klopp is charismatic. He's a proven winner. He can galvanise a crowd through his personality. And he is also a very visible presence. The Liverpool manager watches his players go through their pre-match routine on the pitch. He spends most of a match stood in his technical area, expressing a wide range of emotions as the action unfolds. And when the final whistle goes he again walks onto the turf

to shake the hands of every player and match official before applauding those in the stands who have paid their hard-earned money to be there.

It made for fascinating viewing, even if not all of the match necessarily did. UEFA protocol meant that *You'll Never Walk Alone* was sung before the gladiators entered the arena – their official theme tune takes precedence on such occasions – but the Kop ensured that our new manager, who appeared on the front of the official matchday programme in an iconic Barack Obama pop-art 'Hope poster' design – got to witness the most famous sight in football by belting out an extra chorus. He stood inside his technical area, gazing down towards the Kop end, drinking it all in.

"I've heard so much about Anfield," he said in his pre-match press conference. "We are waiting for this special atmosphere." *You'll Never Walk Alone* gave him a taste of it, but with only 18 Kazan fans having made the arduous 2,000 mile trip from Tatarstan (there were so few of them they flew in on the same plane as the team), Anfield was loud but not at its crackling best. There's more to come, and the same can be said from Klopp's team. A 1-1 draw against a side down to 10 men from the 37th minute wasn't the result we were after, but at least every Kopite knows that their manager goes through exactly the same gamut of emotions as they do during the 90 minutes.

Jürgen Klopp can't help being demonstrative. It's in his blood. And

Pre-Kazan training

First goal of a new era...scored by a German appropriately

those Reds sat in the Paddock and Main Stand saw it up close. After just three minutes he was having words with the fourth official. Soon afterwards, as James Milner forced a corner, he paced up and down his technical area like an expectant father waiting for a baby to be delivered. And, when Emre Can was caught in possession, he shook his head in frustration...only to burst into a spontaneous round of applause when the German midfielder hunted his opponent down and won the ball back.

Kazan played in black and gold. They looked like the 1980s Lotus F1 car that Nigel Mansell and Ayrton Senna drove. And when Marko Devic scored in the 15th minute it put them in pole position. That goal was the first to be registered on Anfield's flashy new scoreboard. The old black one with red lighting, in place since Gerard Houllier was Liverpool boss, has been upgraded for a bright red one with the scoreline in white. The Kazan fans, sat in what used to the Kremlin, sorry, Kemlyn Road stand, must have taken a photo or two of it before it was called into action again in the 37th minute.

Already booked for a studs-up challenge on Alberto Moreno, Kazan skipper Oleg Kuzmin bundled Emre Can over and Austrian referee Robert Schorgenhofer sent him off. Philippe Coutinho curled in a free-kick that just evaded Divock Origi, but the ball flew back across goal off Blagoy Georgiev and Emre Can was lurking to slide it in. Klopp raised both arms aloft before turning to face the Main Stand and fist-pumping the night air. The men who shrewdly appointed him, FSG's John W Henry, Tom Werner and Mike Gordon, smiled and

"HE WALKED DOWN THE TOUCHLINE URGING THE KOP TO CRANK UP THE NOISE"

applauded. Liverpool's first goal of a new era had been scored by a German. It couldn't have been more appropriate.

What followed next, though, was frustration. The Liverpool manager kicked thin air when Kazan were awarded a soft free-kick. He strode

down the touchline clapping his hands in the air when some much-talked about *gegenpressing* saw possession won back. But with chances being passed up early in the second half the Liverpool manager – for just the second time all night – sat next to trusted lieutenant Zeljko Buvac to discuss tactics. Christian Benteke, warming up down the Kop end, was summoned moments later.

Brought on for Coutinho, who was given a hearty man-hug by his new manager as he departed, the Belgian international came closest to getting a winner when his 80th minute shot hit the post just seconds after Klopp had started to walk down the touchline gesticulating towards the Kop with his arms to crank the noise levels up. When *The Fields of Anfield Road* rang out moments later, he turned to the fans and applauded. Perhaps, in that moment, the relationship between Liverpool supporters and their new manager was defined.

When he called for some noise, the crowd responded. When the volume levels were raised, his team almost scored and the Liverpool manager responded to the crowd. Yes, the Redmen didn't emerge victorious, but the positivity that Jürgen Klopp is demanding was evident when the players were clapped off despite a draw. His infectious enthusiasm, and the anticipation of what is to come as he builds his Liverpool team, is beginning to rub off. All in it together? You'd better believe it.

Final whistle and time to take stock

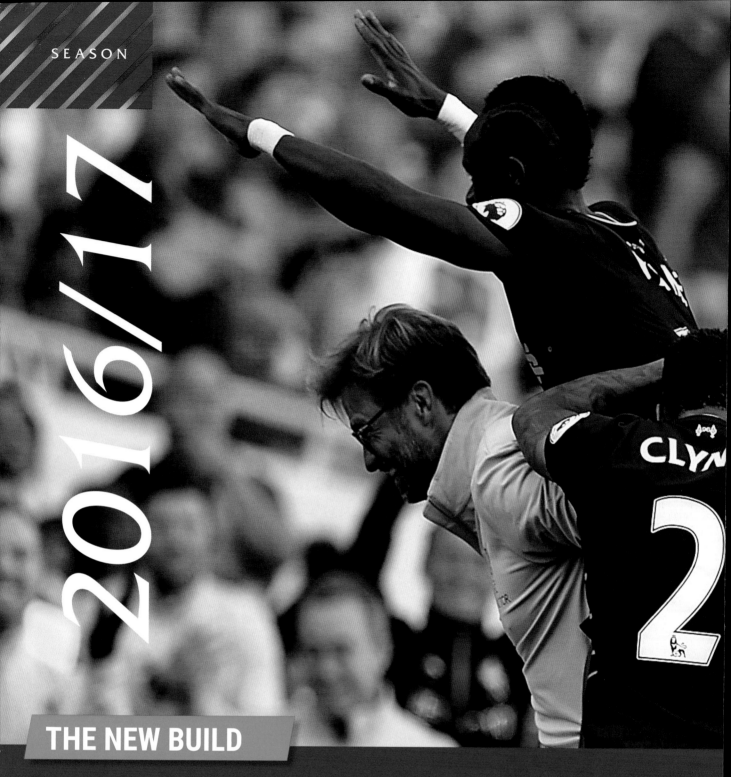

2016/17

THE NEW BUILD

Rebuilding Liverpool off the pitch would be crucial to success on it and the summer of 2016 was vital for Jürgen Klopp. Sadio Mane, Joel Matip and Gini Wijnaldum all became key signings and young Trent Alexander-Arnold was brought through from the Academy.

The Reds also played their first four matches away from home before Anfield's impressive new Main Stand opened, increasing both the capacity and decibel levels.

Liverpool lost just two home Premier League games all season and wouldn't be beaten on their own turf again in the top-flight in front of supporters until late 2022. After defeating Everton and Manchester City 1-0 either side of Christmas, Klopp's new-look team were second in the table, trailing leaders Chelsea by six points, but hit the first real bump in the road by winning only once in two months and exiting both cup competitions.

But 3-1 Anfield successes against Arsenal and Everton perked the Reds up and they won eight of their remaining 12 fixtures during the run-in to secure a return to the Champions League on the last day of the season, an achievement that turned the after-burners on for the Klopp era.

Ahead of his first full season in charge, the official club magazine sat down with Jürgen at Melwood to hear his thoughts...

KICK ASS CLIMB MOUNTAINS STAY COOL

In this exclusive interview Jürgen Klopp reveals what he wants to create at LFC

Jürgen Klopp is talking to LFCTV in the purpose-built studio at Melwood. Last season is dead and gone, not least the finale in Basel: "We all suffered after that final but then you have to say, 'Okay that's it, let's go again'." He describes how the recent trip to America – "I wanted to call it our camp in America rather than an American tour" – was the first chance to get the full first-team squad together and so felt like a second pre-season after the early games back home.

He explains his progressive philosophy towards training and its slow-build intensity: "Nobody wakes up in the morning and says, 'Today I can climb Mount Everest'. But if you climb a number of smaller mountains then you will be ready for it... It's not that we want to run like rabbits, it's about having the opportunity to run like a crazy rabbit if we want to."

And on the Academy's young prospects he's pleased but circumspect: "The world of football and the media all around the game makes it hard to stay a kid as long as you are a kid – and a few of them are still kids. So that's why I have said, 'Let's cool down'. What I can promise is that they are in really good hands and we will try everything we can to bring them through."

And then, away from the camera, he sits down with the club magazine...

WHEN YOU AND YOUR STAFF PREPARE FOR A NEW SEASON, DO YOU BREAK IT INTO CHUNKS AND PLAN FOR SAY, AUGUST-OCTOBER, THEN NOVEMBER-JANUARY, AND SO ON?

At this moment I only know the names of our first five opponents! So we don't plan in a kind of way where we say at this point we will be here, by that point we will be there. I know managers very often say things like this because they are asked about it, saying things like 'After 10 games we will make our first assessment' and so on. I don't think like this, so all I can say is I want to win the first game, and the second, third, fourth and fifth, but it's not like we plan the season in segments.

We prepare pre-season but even then we have to react. When we played Wigan Athletic, for example, two of the players had to play the 90 minutes which was not planned when we were thinking about it a couple of weeks earlier. So we had to change the programme a little bit which is what you always have to do. In the end we are that long in the business that we know what we want to do. That's the cool thing with experience, to really cool down. As a young manager I would think 'Oh my God I can't do this today!' and so you try to force it. Now we are more settled.

Of course the most important time came when all the players – a lot of very good players – returned from the Euros so we had the whole squad together and we could work with them. So that's the way we operate. It makes no sense to plan the season long-term because too often reality takes you out of the race.

DID ANYTHING SURPRISE YOU ABOUT YOUR FIRST SEASON IN ENGLISH FOOTBALL?

A lot of things, for sure, but it feels like a long time ago now. The first impressions were very, very, very positive. In general, the Premier League didn't surprise me because I had read about it before, although the dressing-rooms are much smaller than in Germany – that's very different to be honest! What I can say is that it's a wonderful league in a wonderful country. Since we've been here we have made great experiences with people around the club and in the club and there is a lot of respect between the team.

The image is that it is harder than it actually is. It is intense, very intense, but it's not brutal or something like that. Actually even

"IT MAKES NO SENSE TO PLAN THE SEASON LONG-TERM BECAUSE TOO OFTEN REALITY TAKES YOU OUT OF THE RACE"

if you have watched the Premier League your whole entire life, it's a big difference to really be in it. That's the truth. You have to feel it and only then can you really know it.

I think that we have still to feel a little bit and know a little bit more about it. But it was an intense time during our first few months. We had no routine or anything so nearly everything we did, apart from on the pitch, we did for the first time! So overall I would say the first part of the season was absolutely okay. It could have ended better, of course, but the club is in a good way.

THIS NEW SEASON YOU WILL HAVE THAT GAP BETWEEN FIXTURES – HOW IMPORTANT WILL THAT TIME ON THE TRAINING GROUND BE?

We have to use this time. When we lost the Europa League final, there was absolutely nothing worthwhile about it...just a load of disappointment. In the end the only positive thing about not playing European football this year is that we have more time to train and that is what we have to use, 100 per cent. That's why we need to create a very strong team in the best understanding of the word 'team'.

We need to have competition. We need a situation where the players push themselves and each one pushes the other for each position and wants to be in the team because you have time to recover.

So it's not that you have to change the team a lot between two Saturday games or two Sunday games, it's nothing about rotation. It's about: okay, who is ready now, who is ready to perform how we need to perform in this specific game? And that has to be uncomfortable for the players.

I like to have really a strong bond with the team and between the

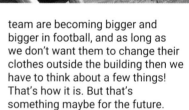

players and all this kind of stuff, but in the end if you really want to step up you sometimes have to kick the ass of your team-mate. That's how it works and this is the kind of atmosphere we have to create.

AFTER YOU SIGNED YOUR NEW CONTRACT, YOU HINTED AT THE POSSIBILITY OF THE CLUB TRAINING ON ONE SITE IN THE FUTURE – THERE WOULD BE OBVIOUS BENEFITS TO SEEING THE YOUNGER PLAYERS DAY-TO-DAY?

I'm sure that [one site] would be better. But even on the occasions when we are all together it's not as

though I am watching a session for the young guys because that's not possible. To be honest, it's like this: the wind situation at Kirkby is not too nice. It's not too 'pro-football'! That means that if we were to go there a lot then there would need to be more trees and buildings, whatever, and that would make it better for everybody.

But, of course, we all love Melwood. It's a wonderful place and 25 years ago it was the best training camp in the Premier League. Now it's still good, really good – there is no issue with it – but a little bit more space here and there would be helpful. The teams around the

team are becoming bigger and bigger in football, and as long as we don't want them to change their clothes outside the building then we have to think about a few things! That's how it is. But that's something maybe for the future.

For the present it's okay. But for the future, I think looking at it would make sense. Everybody's working on it. It's not like I'm forcing it and clapping my hands and saying we cannot be successful when we don't do this.

No, it's about learning about the situation, understanding the situation and then trying to change the right things. That's why I like to be a long-term manager because you can plan things early and then you can use that. To actually build something needs one or two years so when you plan it and build it, you want to be in it, and I like this idea.

I spoke to [Liverpool FC Academy director] Alex Inglethorpe just before the Wigan game and really just said: "Thank you for these boys, it is a big pleasure to have them around." We have had 16, 17 and 18-year-old boys with us in the early part of pre-season and we've had some 19-year-old boys who have gone on loan or been sold, but that

"IF THE FIRST GAME IS OUR BEST OF THE WHOLE SEASON THEN SOMETHING WILL BE WRONG"

is a really good education they have had. Really, really good. So I have to use this.

In the end all the players in our youth at Liverpool need to be ready for professional football. I have no problem with League Two or something like that, but really we want them to be ready for the level of the Championship, maybe not at the beginning but at the end as a minimum. And then the two or three best boys can go through and become Liverpool players. That's a nice dream and one we should all work towards.

YOUR PASSION FOR THE GAME IS CLEAR. WHEN THAT FIRST WEEKEND OF THE SEASON COMES AROUND WILL YOU BE AS EXCITED AS EVER?

Well I haven't played with Liverpool at Arsenal until now because last year the match had been played before I arrived. But yes, I am looking forward to it, of course. It's always like this. I know what everybody will say: that we don't know where we are at this moment. But I am not interested in where we are – only that wherever we are, we do the

best we can. If that [Arsenal] game is the best in the whole season there will be something wrong because that means the rest of our season will see no improvement.

But we need to be as 100-per-cent ready as we can be for that specific day. Then we can work with it and hopefully improve as the season progresses.

Interview: William Hughes

BACK AT EUROPE'S TOP TABLE

Jürgen Klopp's first full season as Liverpool manager saw a return to the UEFA Champions League as the Reds clinched a top-four finish with victory at Anfield on the final day

Among the benefits of having a season without European football was the chance it gave Jürgen Klopp and his staff to spend regular time on the training ground with his squad.

Among those becoming fully acquainted with his methods were his six summer signings.

Sadio Mane, a £30 million capture from Southampton and Gini Wijnaldum, snapped up form Newcastle for a reported £23 million, were the headline arrivals. Joining them were lesser known players such as goalkeepers Loris Karius (Mainz) and Alex Manninger (Augsburg), as well as centre-backs Joel Matip (Schalke) and Ragnar Klavan (Augsburg).

Mane went on to make a major impact and was recognised as Liverpool's star performer of the season by fans and team-mates at the club's 2017 Players' Awards ceremony at Anfield.

In his debut campaign with the Reds, the Senegal international scored 13 Premier League goals in 29 appearances, injecting extra pace and creativity to Jürgen Klopp's side before injury brought a premature conclusion to his debut campaign in April.

Mane - who finished as the team's joint top Premier League scorer with Philippe Coutinho on 13 goals apiece - was voted Player of the Season by supporters in a poll on the club's website, and also secured the accolade of Players' Player of the Season – as chosen by the rest of the Liverpool first team.

The winger made a stunning start to his Reds career in a breathtaking 4-3 win at Arsenal on the season's opening day with as good a debut goal as you could see.

Running onto a chipped Adam Lallana pass down the right, Mane turned the jet-heels on to leave Calum Chambers chasing, cut back inside Nacho Monreal at pace and

curled an absolute beauty off his weaker left foot past Petr Cech into the top corner.

Mane ran off to celebrate with his new manager and there were joyous scenes in the away end.

Mane's goal wasn't the best of the campaign, however. That went to midfielder Emre Can for his incredible overhead kick against Watford, a strike which secured a vital 1-0 win to leave the Reds in third position with three league games remaining.

Fans had hoped that without the distraction of continental football, there may be a chance of success in the domestic cups. However, the Reds were beaten 2-1 by Wolves at Anfield in the fourth-round of the FA Cup having needed a replay to overcome Plymouth Argyle in round-three.

The League Cup seemed like yielding fruit as Klopp chased a second successive final but his side fell short after losing 1-0 home

and away to a Southampton side which had included a certain Virgil van Dijk in the first leg at St Mary's.

However, the Reds' main mission was to return to the Champions League and May gave them four games to secure their spot.

Can's acrobatics at Vicarage Road gave them the perfect start but they faltered at home to Southampton when James Milner's penalty was saved by Fraser Forster and the game ended goalless.

A potentially tricky trip to West Ham United followed but the Reds were imperious at the London Stadium. Midfield magician Coutinho scored twice alongside goals from forwards Daniel Sturridge and Divock Origi to secure a 4-0 victory.

The equation was now simple. Beat Middlesbrough at Anfield and a top four finish was theirs.

Nerves jangled as the Reds failed to break down Steve Agnew's side in the opening 45 minutes but as the opening half ticked into added time, Roberto Firmino teed up Wijnaldum in front of the Kop and the Dutchman rippled the net.

Coutinho and Lallana also found a way past Boro keeper Brad Guzan before the hour mark and Anfield celebrated.

Amid the fist pumping and hugs that greeted the players at the final whistle there was the feeling that this was the start of something special.

Klopp produced a beaming smile post-match as he said: "We worked hard to get the first goal. We got more confident. We then scored from the free-kick and got even more confident.

"The boys then played some fantastic football. I'm really looking forward to next season.

"I think we have created a

wonderful base. The better you're organised, the more you feel free to do special things in offence.

"I'm really happy about this - what a wonderful day."

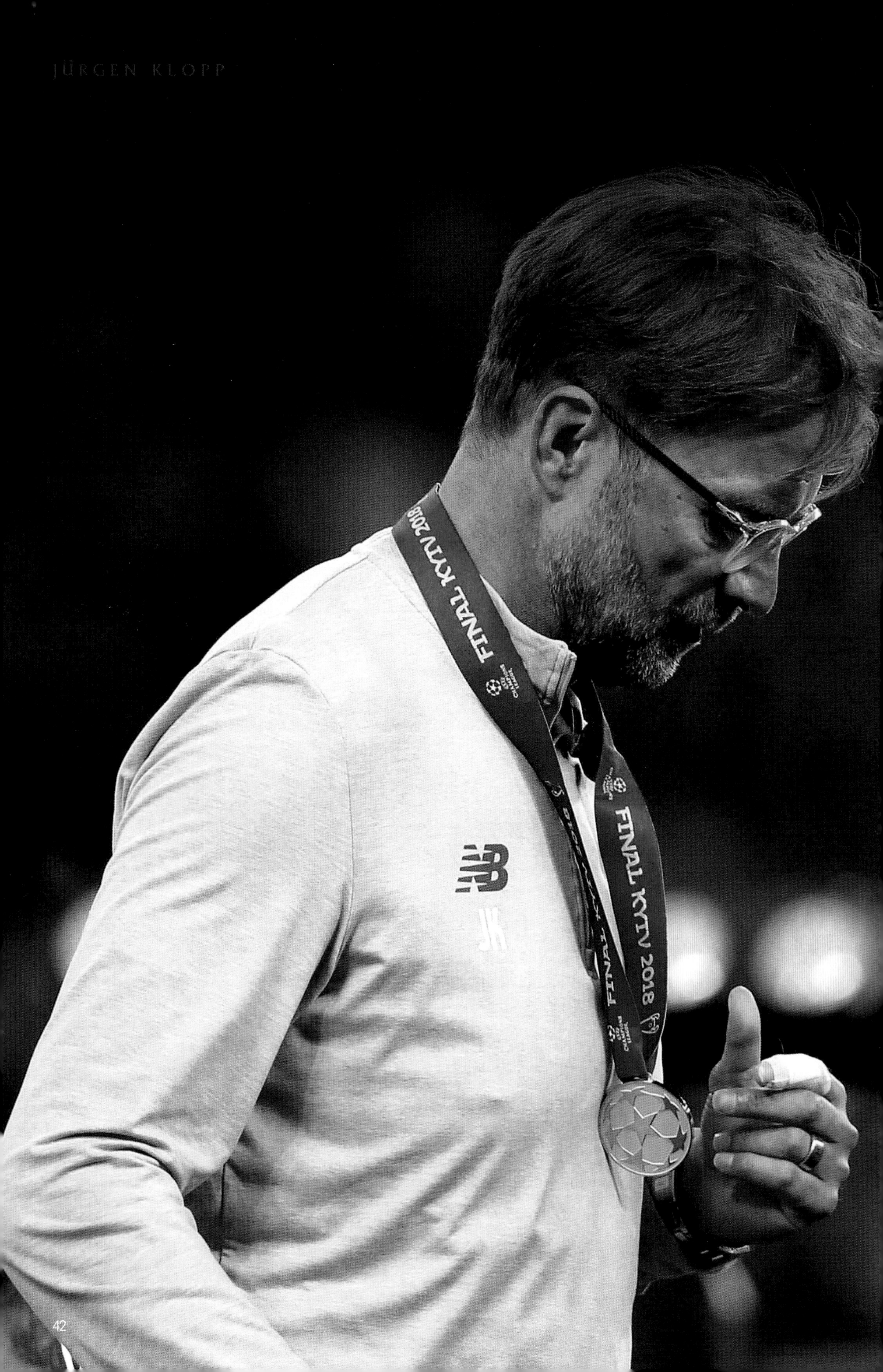
FINAL KYIV 2018
FINAL KYIV 2018

LEARNING CURVE

Mo Salah, Andy Robetson and Alex Oxlade-Chamberlain headlined the summer arrivals and by the time Jürgen Klopp secured the game-changing signing of Virgil van Dijk in January 2018, Liverpool were flying.

Playing in an exciting front-three with Roberto Firmino and Sadio Mane, Salah exceeded expectations by scoring an incredible 44 goals across all competitions and while the Reds' inconsistent away form once again resulted in a fourth-placed finish, Klopp's men were surprise packages in the Champions League.

Liverpool hit seven against Maribor and Spartak Moscow in the group stages and, backed by a partisan, vociferous Anfield, defeated Manchester City and Roma by three-goal margins to reach a first Champions League final since 2007.

The travelling Kop headed to Kyiv, but an injury to Salah after a clash with Sergio Ramos, and two goalkeeping errors by Loris Karius meant it was Real Madrid's night as they triumphed 3-1. A disappointment, yet Klopp and his players would take the experience on board and use it to inspire them to go one better 12 months later.

The final Premier League game of the 2017/18 season left Liverpool needing to beat Brighton & Hove Albion to clinch a top-four finish. In his matchday programme notes, the boss focused on the job in hand

THE MANAGER

"Today will be as tough as any game we've played this season – and we have to do our job"

Good afternoon and welcome back to Anfield for our final Premier League game of the season against Brighton & Hove Albion. I think today the task facing us is very clear. We have work to do – a big job to do.

I welcome Chris Hughton, his players, staff, officials and supporters of Brighton to Anfield for the game.

They might have secured their place in the Premier League again for next season, but they're not coming here for a day out, and therefore today will be as tough as any game we have played this season.

It is very different to last season when we played Middlesbrough needing a similar outcome. Boro were relegated already so came

with a very different feeling – even then, though, the game was incredibly difficult.

The final result maybe means we all forget that for large parts of the first half it was really tough. We had to be so patient and maintain the belief that if we continued to do the right things we would be rewarded. We didn't panic – we stayed calm, we did our job and

the outcome was the result we wanted.

It is hard to find words in English to summarise my admiration for the work Chris Hughton and his staff have done this season. To get promoted is a massive achievement and to then consolidate and establish yourself in the Premier League is, for me, even bigger.

Brighton have achieved this because they have brilliant leadership throughout their club. They've made really smart decisions, stuck together in difficult times and worked hard for each other.

Chris is someone who could easily be considered a contender for the manager of the season because of how he has guided his side this season. He is so calm and dignified, both in the dugout and in how he presents himself publicly. He is a wonderful role-model for coaches and managers in England and I love that his work is recognised.

I saw their win against Manchester United and of course in the aftermath much of the focus is on Manchester not winning, but this is so unfair. Brighton were exceptional and seemed very fresh and very bright.

This is our warning today: Brighton still have many miles in the tank and we need to be ready to work harder than they work, and fight harder than they fight. It is that simple.

But as much as we respect Brighton we come into the game with confidence and with belief that we can finish our season in the best way possible.

Belief has been central to so many of the positive things we have done this season. Belief and confidence are completely different to arrogance and complacency. We have to value and recognise our strengths and then execute the plan that plays to them.

We have been pushed to the limit in recent weeks with the intensity of what we have been doing. This is not an excuse – it is information, it is a fact. We have lost important players to injuries through bad luck and the knock-on effect has meant more physical and mental pressure on the lads who have to keep going and keep going.

But I say 'no excuse' because this intensity is what we want. It's intense because it matters. Also, ahead of today we have had a full seven days to prepare and be ready and this undoubtedly will help us in our approach.

I said after Chelsea – and it has been repeated by the players – that today is a cup final and it is. And that's not to add unnecessary pressure, it's just to highlight the opportunity.

Today is about opportunity. A Champions League place for next season and all that comes with it is within our grasp if we want to take it. Like any cup final, it will not be given or presented to us. We have to go and do our job, all of us. But in a season where the competition in the Premier League has been of the highest quality ever and the intensity of the competition the highest ever, we can achieve one of our major objectives by winning today.

That really is the start and end of any team-talk, I can tell you.

Finally, I wish to thank our supporters for everything they have given us since August. It's almost easy to forget now that we started this campaign by going to Hoffenheim, so our journey has been incredibly intense from moment one.

This has been a journey shared by our supporters and, unlike us in the team, their travel, accommodation and tickets are not laid on for them.

The players talk a lot about their admiration for the supporters because many of their own family and friends share the experiences of our fans. They share the journey times, the delays, the cost and sacrifice of time to prioritise supporting this great club.

I love that from our captain to the youngest player in the squad our boys recognise that representing these supporters is a massive privilege and I love that there is a shared appreciation in this moment of each other. Players and supporters unified and together.

Thank you for the amazing support this season and I hope that there are at least two more great memories for us to share before it is time for summer.

You'll Never Walk Alone
Jürgen

JÜRGEN KLOPP

HAPPY BIRTHDAY LFC

CELEBRATING 125 YEARS
OF THE LIVERPOOL WAY

The story of Liverpool's 125th season

A special anniversary campaign didn't disappoint as the Reds secured another top four finish, introduced a new colossus in defence and reached a Champions League final

Liverpool's 125th league season began with a 3-3 draw at Watford. Among the scorers was summer signing Mohamed Salah who would become a regular fixture on the scoresheet in a red shirt!

The first home league game, a 1-0 win over Crystal Palace, saw another new recruit, Andy Robertson, enjoy a fine debut.

The Reds then thrashed Arsenal 4-0 at Anfield with Sadio Mane becoming only the third player to score in the first three PL games of a season for LFC after Robbie Fowler (1994/95) and Daniel Sturridge (2013/14).

September's home game against Burnley was a special one as LFC marked 125 years since its very first game, a friendly against Rotherham Town on Thursday 1 September 1892. Among a host of 125-themed activities is a commemorative mosaic and schoolchildren and Reds legends forming a 'guard of honour' around the pitch.

October brought a 7-0 win at Maribor in a Champions League group game – a new club-record away European win.

Ahead of the home game against Southampton, on 18 November, Liverpool unveiled a unique work of art at the new Anfield store, commissioned to commemorate the 125th anniversary. Sports artist

Jamie Cooper distilled the past, present and future on a stunning three-metre oil-on-canvas entitled 'LFC Dream Scene'. It brings together 19 of Liverpool's greatest servants and a lucky young competition winner in one magical moment in time. The artwork also featured on a special gatefold cover for the official matchday programme.

December, busy? Just a tad. The first of eight games in the month brought a 5-1 victory at Brighton & Hove Albion which moved the Reds into the top four of the Premier League for the first time since August.

A 7-0 trouncing of Spartak Moscow in the Champions League at Anfield saw captain-for-the-

night Philippe Coutinho net his first LFC hat-trick as the Reds sealed their place in the last 16 in style with a goal-count of 23-7 on aggregate over the six group games.

A 5-0 home win over Swansea City on Boxing Day brought a first Reds goal for local boy Trent Alexander-Arnold. "Every lad dreams of scoring at the Kop-end under the floodlights, and especially with it coming off the bar and going in!," the no66 told reporters afterwards.

January saw the club make their record signing and Virgil van Dijk marked his Liverpool debut in some style - by scoring the winner in a Merseyside derby! The centre-back's Kop-end header gave the

46

Reds a 2-1 win over Everton in an FA Cup third-round clash.

Salah was named African Player of the Year for 2017 and starred as the Reds became the first team of the season to beat Manchester City in the Premier League, running out 4-3 winners in an Anfield thriller.

February saw the Reds inflict FC Porto's heaviest-ever home defeat in Europe as Mane hit a hat-trick in a 5-0 victory at the Estadio do Dragao as Liverpool built a healthy first-leg advantage in their round-of-16 tie.

March was another month of solid progress as the Reds won three out of their four Premier League games with Salah scoring four times in a 5-0 home win against Watford.

Sensational Champions League performances against Manchester City and AS Roma made April a memorable month. The Reds took control of their quarter-final tie against City and semi-final clash with the Italian side by building three-goal first leg advantages at Anfield backed by a vociferous home support.

Salah's sensational season was recognised by his fellow professionals as he was named as the PFA Player of the Year.

Moving into May a 1-0 defeat at

Chelsea meant the Reds needed to win their final game of the season against Brighton and they produced a first-class display against the Seagulls to secure fourth position for a second successive season.

Prior to the game Salah was named as the Football Writers' Footballer of the Year, becoming the sixth Liverpool man to win both the PFA and FWA awards in the same season. His strike in the Reds' 3-0 victory also saw him claim the Premier League's Golden Boot award after he finished as the division's top scorer with 32 goals.

And so to Kyiv. It wasn't to be as Real Madrid secured a third consecutive success in the tournament to win their 13th European Cup but the travelling Reds created an incredible atmosphere and returned home optimistic about what the future would hold under Klopp.

"In all the finals that my teams had played before, we played better football but we lost," said the manager. "So, we have to learn to win finals and

we've won a few; not Champions League finals, but a few others. We are now more experienced and that's probably good."

Indeed it was!

Alisson Becker, Fabinho, Naby Keita and Xherdan Shaqiri were Jürgen Klopp's major summer signings and with the two Brazilians seriously enhancing the spine of the team, Liverpool had one of the best campaigns in the club's entire history.

They lost just one Premier League game all season and clocked up a club-record 97 points, but that defeat came against Pep Guardiola's Manchester City at the Etihad Stadium and was enough for the Mancunians to edge the title race as both clubs took levels of consistency to new heights.

Yet the Reds were fighting for glory on two fronts and after Roberto Firmino's late winner against PSG and Alisson's late save against Napoli proved pivotal in getting out of a difficult group, the Reds beat Bayern Munich in the Allianz Arena and saw off Porto to set up a semi-final against Barcelona.

Beaten 3-0 at Camp Nou, Klopp's side created Anfield's greatest European night of all when they stunned Lionel Messi and co with a 4-0 comeback win and it was the scorer of the decisive goal, Divock Origi, who also secured a 2-0 win against Tottenham Hotspur in the final in Madrid after Mo Salah converted an early penalty.

Jürgen Klopp and Liverpool FC were Champions of Europe.

SEASON

2018/19

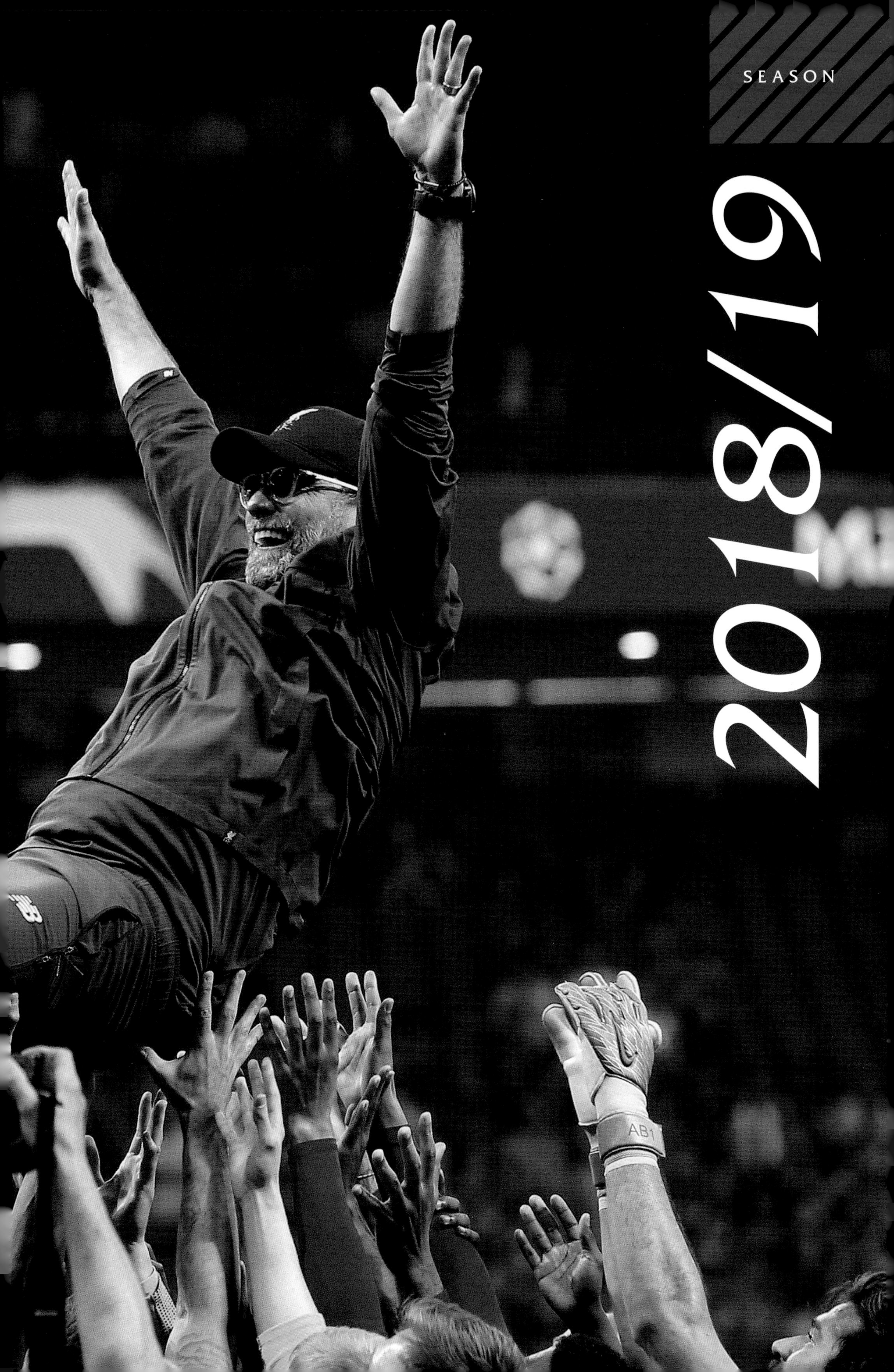

The official matchday programme for the UEFA Champions League quarter-final v FC Porto in April 2019 took us on a pictorial journey of Jürgen's managerial career via Mainz and Borussia Dortmund to the Reds

JÜRGEN

MAINZ MAN: after more than 300 appearances and 50 goals in eleven seasons as a player for FSV Mainz 05, Jürgen is appointed as manager with his first task saving the *Karnevalsverein* (Carnival club) from relegation from Bundesliga 2, eventually leading them into the top flight after some near-misses. Facing the Reds for the first time in a pre-season friendly in 2006, his team put five past Liverpool at the Bruchwegstadion. After seven years as boss, a new challenge awaits in the north of Germany...

BEATING THE BAVARIANS 1: a beaming Klopp on media duties during another seven-year stint as manager, now at Borussia Dortmund. Successfully breaking Bayern Munich's dominance, he leads the Yellow and Blacks to back-to-back league titles in 2011 and 2012, as well as one German Cup and two German Super Cups as Borussia boss. Of their success, Klopp once remarked: "We have a bow and arrow and if we aim well, we can hit the target. The problem is that Bayern has a bazooka. But then Robin Hood was quite successful."

WALL OF ACCLAIM: Dortmund's Yellow Wall – their own version of the Kop with its countless flags and banners – give their thanks to their outgoing manager who takes charge of his final game at the Westfalenstadion in May 2015. A quirk of his three management jobs is that each club has adopted You'll Never Walk Alone as its anthem. Perhaps inevitable then that after a four-month holiday he takes up his current post...

SUIT UP: it's Jürgen's first home game in charge of Liverpool Football Club, and the only game here so far where he's worn a suit! The match ends 1-1 against Rubin Kazan, with Klopp remarking: "When you come for the first time to a new house you have a present. I am not quite satisfied with mine!" There would be many a more memorable European occasion to come, even that season. "We will try to start playing emotional football because I think this is important at Anfield," Jürgen promised. Fair to say he's delivered on that!

KLOPPO HUGS: sharing the love after a resounding 6-1 win at Southampton in the League Cup with fan favourite Lucas en route to a first final in charge of the Reds. He later says: "I'm really demanding to be honest, and I really want a lot of them. When you can really see how they fight, with the last drop of fuel in their machine, the easiest thing to do is hug them."

SPECS-Y FOOTBALL: a manic afternoon's work, still in the infancy of the manager's reign, sees a topsy-turvy encounter at Norwich City finish 5-4 to the Reds, who at one point had trailed 3-1. Klopp's glasses are smashed in the celebrations following Adam Lallana's 95th-minute winner, with the boss joking afterwards: "They were absolutely broken! In the picture, I have them in my hands. It was Christian Benteke who did it. So don't kill my glasses or otherwise you will be sold!"

TOUCHING TRIBUTES: on the eve of the 27th anniversary of Hillsborough both sets of supporters sing YNWA and hold up mosaics in tribute to the 96 before kick-off. The respect and solidarity between supporters earns a FIFA award, with Klopp reacting after one of Anfield's greatest ever nights and comebacks: "The atmosphere was the best I have ever experienced. It should serve as an example to everyone about how supporters can influence a team and influence a game. Of course, this award honours both sets of supporters and the respect shown by our friends from Dortmund was absolutely typical of the world-class values that club upholds. I know we won the match and the tie, but I think everyone inside Anfield that night and watching at home – whether they were wearing red or yellow and black – knows that football can be very proud of how they represented their club."

SEVILLE FAWLTY: the quizzical expression on Jurgen's face sums up what we're all feeling as a 1-0 lead quickly turns into a 3-1 UEFA Europa League final defeat in Basel (see what we didn't do there). It delays a return to the Champions League for another season after Daniel Sturridge's sublime opener is overturned after the break, but that would be put right in the following campaign. "After the game we were obviously down but when we got back to the hotel, the manager had something different about him," recalls Jordan Henderson. "He felt it was the start of something, something he could take forward."

MOMENT OF GINI-OUS: Jürgen keeps his emotions in check as best he can as a tense Anfield erupts as a Wijnaldum strike in first-half stoppage-time gives the Reds the upper hand towards Champions League qualification. Relegated Middlesbrough are eventually swept aside 3-0 as Liverpool finish fourth and one point ahead of Arsenal, proving how big a result that opening-day victory at the Emirates was. A tricky tie against Hoffenheim would need to be negotiated now, just the start of an incredible European campaign to follow.

GOAL RUSH: a 2016/17 opening-day encounter at Arsenal ends 4-3 to the Reds after some sizzling attacking football sees Liverpool score three times early in the second half, the pick of the bunch a debut drive from Sadio Mane. Ragnar Klavan and Gini Wijnaldum also play for LFC for the first time while future signing Alex Oxlade-Chamberlain nets for the Gunners. These celebrations after Mane's contribution are more than a hint of the thrilling ride to come.

CLEAN-SHEET CASILLAS: last season's clash with FC Porto here at Anfield ends goalless with the competition's all-time leading appearance-maker shaking hands with the boss after excelling in the visitor's goal. Thankfully the job was done in the first leg, the 5-0 aggregate win sealing a quarter-final tie with Manchester City. The Kop are famed for applauding opposition keepers when they defend the Kop goal and this does not go unnoticed by the Spanish stopper. "I would like to thank the Liverpool fans for that lovely detail," Iker says. "Applauding a player from the opposite team does not happen very often."

SIXTH SENSE: 'I see Red people' reads one of the many LFC banners as tens of thousands of Liverpool supporters' unforgettable European adventure ends for another year, sadly in defeat in the Kyiv final. But they and Jürgen Klopp are particularly buoyant about the better times that may lie ahead, the manager later remarking: "In a final you need to have a bit of luck and we didn't have it. They had luck in different situations and we didn't. They scored a bicycle-kick, come on!"

HOLY TRINITY: as part of a famous Bill Shankly quote goes, "At a football club, there's a holy trinity – the players, the manager and the supporters," and the current boss has certainly been instrumental in bringing the players and supporters closer together. Ensuring the Reds play in friendlies in the North West ahead of global pre-season tours means more fans get the chance to see their heroes in action, with this season's Anfield warm-up match against Torino a treat for local fans getting the same opportunities as overseas support in getting up and close with the players and staff for photos and autographs. "We will do things around the game we usually don't do, these things that aren't possible in a purely competitive game," said Klopp. "I hope we see us all together because from my point-of-view we want to do things like that more often."

HAPPY BIRTHDAY TO YOU! another new tradition introduced by the boss is to celebrate a birthday with players and staff standing in a circle to serenade the birthday boy with a song and applause. Simon Mignolet is the recipient of the new ritual in the photo here.

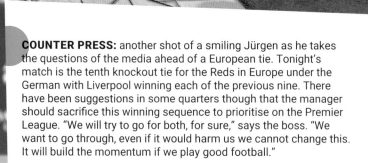

COUNTER PRESS: another shot of a smiling Jürgen as he takes the questions of the media ahead of a European tie. Tonight's match is the tenth knockout tie for the Reds in Europe under the German with Liverpool winning each of the previous nine. There have been suggestions in some quarters though that the manager should sacrifice this winning sequence to prioritise on the Premier League. "We will try to go for both, for sure," says the boss. "We want to go through, even if it would harm us we cannot change this. It will build the momentum if we play good football."

BEATING THE BAVARIANS 2: last time out in the UEFA Champions League sees Liverpool seal a hugely satisfying result in Munich to ensure the Reds were in the hat for this game tonight. The boss sums it up: "Scoring three goals here is massive and a big step for us, a big, big step. We will see what we can do with it but it is a fantastic sign. We set a mark for LFC tonight that we are back on the international landscape as a football club. I am really happy about the result. I knew we had a chance but I didn't expect it would happen, but the boys made it happen and it was really brilliant. I think this club deserves recognition and awareness again. We are back – that's good, we have a lot to learn but we are back."

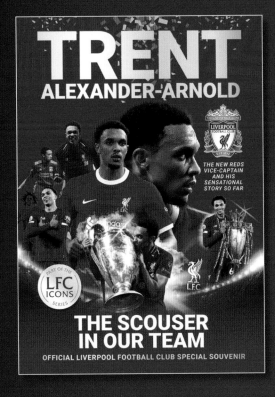

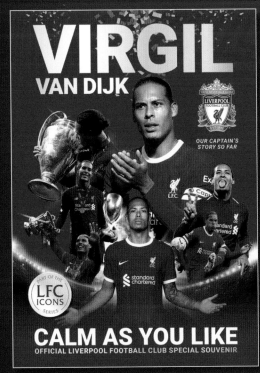
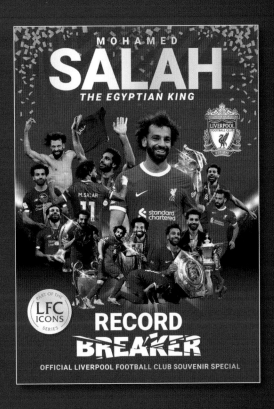

JÜRGEN KLOPP
★★★★★★ *BABY!*

The boss spoke to the press in Estadio Metropolitano an hour after watching his side lift the European Cup and to LFCTV while on the open-top bus parading through the rammed streets of Liverpool. Here's what the delighted Reds' manager had to say...

JÜRGEN ON... WHAT WAS DIFFERENT ABOUT THE 2019 CHAMPIONS LEAGUE FINAL IN MADRID COMPARED TO KYIV 2018

The result, obviously. We all spoke about it a lot, I played much more finals than I won, we always played better football. Tonight it was a big challenge for both teams to deal with the three weeks [between games] because you never have a period with three weeks and no game. So keep the rhythm or get the rhythm back actually. Then obviously it was different circumstances for two English teams, it was pretty warm. You saw it was a fight. A final is about the result and we need to make this experience a little bit longer or more often than others. Tonight the boys showed it, the resilience and everything you need to block the decisive balls.

Ali had to make a few saves, he of course played a sensational game, absolutely, he looked completely unbeatable pretty much. That helped us. We scored goals in the right moment. Usually I always sit here a bit earlier and have to explain how you can lose this game. This time, I don't want to explain why we won it, I only want to enjoy that we won

it. All the rest is not important. It's for all the people around the world, in the stadium, they are with us and they are now celebrating like crazy.

I feel mostly relief, to be honest, relief for my family actually because they are pretty close to me as you can imagine and the last six times we always flew on holiday with a silver medal, that doesn't feel too cool. This is completely different this year. It's for them as well, that's great. It's for the supporters of course, but for our owners as well because they never put real pressure on us, they appreciate the development, they see the steps we make. It's for them as well. For the players, we were all pretty much crying on the pitch because it was so emotional, it was so big, it means so much to us.

On the other hand and I should have probably said this first of all, I know how Tottenham feel in this moment better than anybody else in the world. They played a sensational season as well and they would have deserved it as well, but tonight we scored the goals in the right moment. I told Poch already after the game that he should be really proud of what they did this year as well.

JÜRGEN ON... THE MOST SATISFYING THING ABOUT BEING CHAMPIONS OF EUROPE

I'm happy for the boys. You know what people said about a couple of players of this team. Jordan Henderson is captain of the Champions League winner 2019 – that's satisfying actually. That Millie did it at the age of 33. They are all very important. But I can say again, without Millie's dressing-room talks before the game – with a non-native speaking manager – I think it would not be possible. It's so important.

All the things they did during the weeks, how they lifted when we had little downs, it's just incredible. Tonight is really emotional, that's my main feeling, it's overwhelming, all that stuff. It feels really good but I'm much calmer than I thought I would be when it finally happened. It was not important to me to touch the cup or whatever. I loved the pictures when the boys had it, I loved it when I saw a few faces in the stands. That gave me everything I need. Tomorrow, going to Liverpool and having something to celebrate, that's big and I'm really looking forward to that.

"WITHOUT MILLIE'S DRESSING-ROOM TALKS BEFORE THE GAME – WITH A NON-NATIVE SPEAKING MANAGER – I THINK IT WOULD NOT BE POSSIBLE. IT'S SO IMPORTANT "

JÜRGEN ON... WHAT WINNING THE CHAMPIONS LEAGUE MEANS TO HIM PERSONALLY

We spoke two days ago about my 'unlucky' career somehow. When I hear it I think, 'Yeah, people could see it like this', but I don't feel it to be honest because I always see the way to a final as well because that's of course important for me. I think my life is much better than I ever expected it, so winning something is good, it's cool, but it's for all the other people. I'm not so much in it, I'm much more really in development but I get it, we have to win things, so for us it's really important that people don't ask now all the time about not winning or winning things.

Now we won something and we will carry on. We want to win things, 100 per cent. I've said it, this is only the start for this group. It's still a wonderful age group, they all have the best times in their careers ahead of them so that's big. For me, I'm really happy. I have a lot of silver medals and now I have a golden one so it'll be next to the silver medals in my house and that's cool. But mostly I'm happy for all the other people. When you see it now in the dressing-room, everybody feels it but you don't really know what to do with it. But tomorrow I'm really sure when we drive through the city, then we all will realise what these boys have done and that's the best moment, for sure.

“ 97 POINTS IN THE LEAGUE IS INCREDIBLE AND WINNING THE CHAMPIONS LEAGUE – THAT'S AN UNBELIEVABLY LONG WAY TO GO AND WE DID IT, THAT'S INCREDIBLE **”**

JÜRGEN ON... NEXT YEAR'S FINAL BEING IN ISTANBUL

I told UEFA already: we will be there! Give me a few minutes! We know that sometimes we carry the burden of history and making Istanbul happen again will be a target I would say, but it will be difficult. By the way, a second ago I spoke to Pep Guardiola on the phone because we had a physio who worked for Man City at the beginning of the season. We promised each other already that we will kick our butts again next year. We will go for everything and we'll see if we get something, that's it.

JÜRGEN ON... THE WIN BEING A COLLECTIVE EFFORT

That's absolutely OK, I like that actually. So, my job is to take all the responsibility and I like that actually because it gives my players the freedom to play football. That's how I understand it. Sometimes it would be easier to understand it in a different way but that's how I understand it. Tonight I am so happy for the players and I'm happy really for my family, and there will be a moment when I'm completely overwhelmed for myself maybe. But look at my coaches, what we all did during the year to try to make the next step. So when we started in Evian in the training camp, bringing these players and knowing they need time but we had to win football games from the start, it was difficult.

But it feels so good: 97 points, now you can say it, 97 points in the league is incredible and winning the Champions League – that's an unbelievably long way to go and we did it, that's incredible. But after the final last year, when we came home to Liverpool, it was not cool but one of my friends is a singer and my assistant coach we sang a song: 'We saw the European Cup, Madrid had all the f*****g luck, we swear we'll keep on being cool, we'll bring it back to Liverpool'. Nobody thought in that moment it would happen. In that moment it was only to lift our mood a little bit and now it happened actually, so now we have to think about what we will sing tonight because obviously it means something.

DELIVERED WHAT HE SAID

Jürgen Klopp's European champions spent the season gathering more silverware and the UEFA Super Cup was soon added to the collection, Sadio Mane scoring twice in a 2-2 draw against Chelsea in Istanbul before new goalkeeper Adrian emerged as the hero in the penalty shoot-out.

The Reds also made history in Qatar when a goal by Roberto Firmino against Flamengo made Liverpool FIFA Club World Cup champions for the first time, but it was in the Premier League that Klopp enjoyed his greatest triumph of all.

Liverpool won 26 and drew one of their opening 27 games to smash all kinds of records and streak clear of the rest only for the coronavirus pandemic to put the season - and life for everyone - on hold.

A nervy wait followed and when football finally resumed in June it was behind closed doors, but the Reds' first league title since 1990, and first in the Premier League era, was inevitable and secured with a record seven games left to play.

Klopp and his players lifted the trophy on the Kop as, finally, Liverpool were champions for a 19th time.

2019/20

In Qatar during December 2019, Jürgen became the first Liverpool FC manager to win the FIFA Club World Cup, one of many memorable moments of his LFC reign featured in the official club book I Feel Fine

LIVERPOOL > DOHA
4500KM

WE WON IT IN QATAR

"WE ARE REALLY HAPPY TO BE HERE AND THAT WE BRING THE TROPHY TO OUR CITY, TO OUR CLUB"
– ALISSON BECKER

> **"I SAID BEFORE THE GAME I DON'T KNOW EXACTLY HOW IT WOULD FEEL. NOW I CAN SAY IT'S OUTSTANDING, ABSOLUTELY SENSATIONAL. I'M SO PROUD OF THE BOYS AND IT COULDN'T BE BETTER"**
>
> **– JÜRGEN KLOPP**

FIFA CLUB WORLD CUP QATAR 2019™

Monterrey, Flamengo, we're the greatest team by far, we're the mighty Liverpool, we won it in Qatar, we won it in Qatar...'

Jürgen Klopp's European champions headed off to the gulf state in December 2019 intent on becoming the first Liverpool side to win the FIFA Club World Cup, but with Jordan Henderson playing at the back as Joe Gomez was the only fit centre-half, and Adam Lallana deputising for the injured Fabinho in the holding midfield role, the Redmen faced a tricky semi-final against Mexican side Monterrey.

Naby Keita's early goal was cancelled out and it was only in the 91st minute, when Trent Alexander-Arnold crossed to fellow substitute Roberto Firmino, that the Reds booked a place in the final against Flamengo. A win for the Brazilians, who had beaten Liverpool 3-0 in Tokyo in the 1981 Intercontinental Cup, would complete a treble to make it their greatest ever season, but Virgil van Dijk returned from illness and it was to be Bobby's night.

The final was in extra-time when he received a pull-back from Sadio Mane, delayed his shot to wrongfoot the goalkeeper and slotted home. Off came Firmino's shirt in celebration and when the final whistle blew the mighty Reds of Liverpool were club world champions for the first time, adding another prestigious honour to the list.

After being confirmed as Premier League champions for the first time, Jürgen used his programme notes for the game v Aston Villa to say he didn't want his team to stop

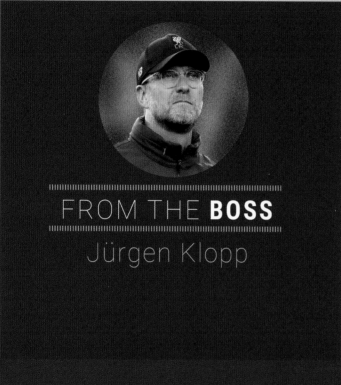

FROM THE **BOSS**
Jürgen Klopp

Hello to you, wherever you are when you read this, ahead of our Premier League fixture against Aston Villa.

Because of the obvious challenges in the region, country and world right now, I am writing this column well before we travel to play Manchester City and therefore cannot reflect upon anything that has happened for us or our opponents since then.

I welcome Dean Smith, the players and officials of Aston Villa to Anfield today. It seems like a lifetime ago that we first met this season, but even given all that time the memories of that unbelievably tough game remain.

Dean has done a fantastic job and his story really is one that makes your heart glow with warmth. He has always been successful whichever club he has managed. And then to have earned the opportunity to lead a club that means so much to him is always good to see.

Their promotion last season was such a big achievement and if I'm being honest the level of performance I see from his side this season says to me they deserve to be in a better position than they find themselves at the moment.

WE HAVE ACHIEVED MUCH TOGETHER BUT WE CANNOT PRESS THE PAUSE BUTTON FOR EVEN ONE MOMENT

We know from the game at Villa Park that they can match any side on their day because of their quality and organisation, so we must be ready to work as hard as in any game this season.

Also, my love goes to Dean for the loss he suffered this season, with his father passing. I was deeply touched by the tribute Aston Villa paid to him and I can only imagine how proud he must have been of his son, achieving something so important and special with the club they both cherish.

Turning back to us, of course this is the first column I have written since we were confirmed champions. I will go into this more ahead of the final home game, because I think it is important to emphasise the need for focus on what we still have ahead of us.

One of our defining features, as a team, has been to embody the spirit of the line in the supporters' song Allez Allez Allez when they declare 'We're never gonna stop'. I love everything about that line.

This team has embraced that mentality. We have achieved much together but we cannot press the pause button for even one moment. It is important to savour and enjoy the special moments. It is not allowed that we don't recognise these shared experiences. But it is possible, if you have the mindset, to do both: enjoy the 'now' but be in a hungry and greedy mood for more in the future.

I keep getting asked about 'dynasty' and 'dominance' and I really don't like it. One headline since we came back wrongly suggested it was our plan to build a dynasty. I never said this and never would.

Let's keep to our values – and that is to be humble.

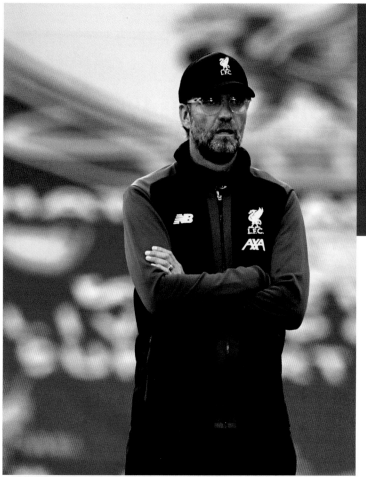

If we remain humble, as individuals, as a team and as a club, we can achieve so much more together. And being humble isn't about not celebrating.

Trust me. I am a big fan of celebrating like crazy.

Humility is about how you approach your work. For me it's about recognising that I need to improve as a coach and a leader and find ways to be better. For my players it is about being prepared to work even harder than you have before. Titles don't make players better. Their day-to-day work does that. Their attitude does that, their ability to be humble and accept they are not perfect and can be better.

And for our fans it's about recognising that their role will always be critical to everything we do and

I CANNOT WAIT FOR THESE MOMENTS WHEN WE WILL CELEBRATE TOGETHER – BUT THE TIME IS NOT NOW

they need to keep being our energy source.

On that subject, once again our supporters are not able to be at Anfield today but I want to talk about them because not only have they played a vital role in us winning the Premier League, many of them have also responded magnificently to the crisis that the world is in.

Last week I had a Zoom call with some of the Liverpool and Everton fans who worked together to produce personal protective equipment when there was a national shortage.

What they have done is unbelievable. To want to respond in that way is more than good enough in itself, but to have the ingenuity, determination and leadership to make it happen on a mass scale is so incredible that I could not possibly find the words to do it justice.

I felt privileged to speak to them. They are heroes. By finding ingenious ways to support our community locally they have undoubtedly helped save lives and keep people safe. This, to me, is the spirit of Liverpool. It is why I have come to love the city and its people.

I also want to pay tribute to the supporters who volunteered to deliver food to some of the most vulnerable members of our community. I am told that this was organised by the Spirit Of Shankly and there is no doubt that by acting in this way they lived up to the spirit of one of the greatest men of all.

But it is knowing that so many of you have done so much at a time of great suffering that made last Friday's events at the Pier Head so disappointing. I am a football manager, not a judge, and I have the same ability to make the mistakes of a human being as everyone else, so what I am saying should be taken in this spirit. But I also have to be clear: what we saw was not good for Liverpool the city or Liverpool the club.

The same people who were vulnerable when supporters were manufacturing PPE and delivering food are still vulnerable now. We cannot allow all of this brilliant work to go to waste because some

have decided that they either cannot wait for a celebration or that COVID-19 is no longer a threat. If we do this, people – our people – will be put at risk.

We need you to stay at home as much as possible, not because we want to stop your enjoyment, but because we care for everyone who lives in this city and other places beyond.

It is a strange thing for me to say because it goes against everything that I usually would say, but right now we do not want to see you at stadiums and we don't want to see you gathering to celebrate. I say this out of a sense of care and for no other reason.

When the time comes you will be back at Anfield and we will also be able to celebrate together. I cannot wait for these moments, but the time is not now. We must respect the virus like we would respect any opponent. Anything else puts all of us at risk.

If we can all follow the example of our supporters who have put others first, we will not go wrong and we owe it to ourselves to do that.

You'll Never Walk Alone
Jürgen

As the Reds prepared to lift their first Premier League trophy, the boss used his programme notes v Chelsea to stress his regret that the fans couldn't be at Anfield to celebrate with them

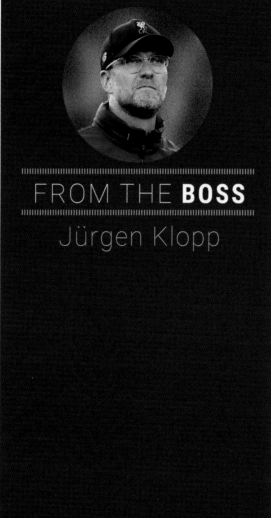

FROM THE **BOSS**

Jürgen Klopp

Hello to you wherever you are when you read this, ahead of our final Premier League fixture at Anfield this season against Chelsea.

I welcome Frank Lampard, his players, staff and officials of the visitors to our home.

What a job Frank has done this season. We have played them three times already this campaign, in three different competitions and each time the games have been so close and so tight. They are already starting to reflect their manager's personality in how they approach the game and it's very easy to see they are heading in the right direction.

Wonderful players, some really smart and ambitious recruitments made, superb leadership in the manager's office. Chelsea have been a real challenge this season and will be even stronger next.

Moving to ourselves, as much as the 90 minutes is the main focus, I cannot ignore the hugely significant night we are about to experience as a team and as a club.

Yes, as always the game comes first and all our attention and energies will be on that. We have a responsibility to the competition, of course, but also ourselves. We have enjoyed a wonderful season and it is important we finish it in a manner fitting the level of achievement. This is something within our control. As we have all season, we set our own standards and try to exceed them.

I know I won't need to remind the players of this, because they are smart and hungry and they know the job to do.

When the game is done, we will be recognised

WE HAVE ENJOYED A WONDERFUL SEASON AND IT IS IMPORTANT WE FINISH IT IN A FITTING MANNER

as Champions of England. The first time since 1990 for this incredible football club.

I know we live in a world where 'what's next' often means the 'here and now' isn't savoured as much as it should be. No sooner had we been confirmed Champions – on the night when tonight's opponents had beaten Manchester City – and the questions were coming about 'legacy' and 'winning more'.

It is so important to enjoy the wonderful moments when they come. And this is one of those.

I don't normally like referencing the length of time Liverpool has endured before claiming this title, because so often when working to clinch it my message was to ignore the weight of that gap. Last season, when we came so close, I said to the players afterwards that this was not the 29th attempt for them – for us, it was our first proper one. I also told them I loved them, appreciated them and was so proud to be able to call myself their manager.

Everything I said in the dressing-room after Wolves at home last season when we came so close but ultimately could only achieve runners up, applies now but even more so.

I could not love this group of players more. I could not appreciate them more. I could not be more proud of them.

This achievement is their achievement. Their focus. Their dedication. Their talent. Their hunger. That's what has delivered this title. They sacrificed, individually and collectively, and they have their rewards.

This group of players are giants for what they achieved. They have earned every bit of praise and adulation that has come their way.

Tonight is their moment as a team and even though it is happening in unique circumstances, the magnitude of what they have delivered stands alongside some of the greatest sides ever to grace our home.

Typically I have used a lot of words there to express a sentiment I could have summed up in just two: 'thank you'. Thank you to the most incredible football team any manager could be privileged to lead.

The same applies to two other special groups, my remarkable staff and the Liverpool supporters.

This is a moment in the column where I have to show discipline, because if I start naming too

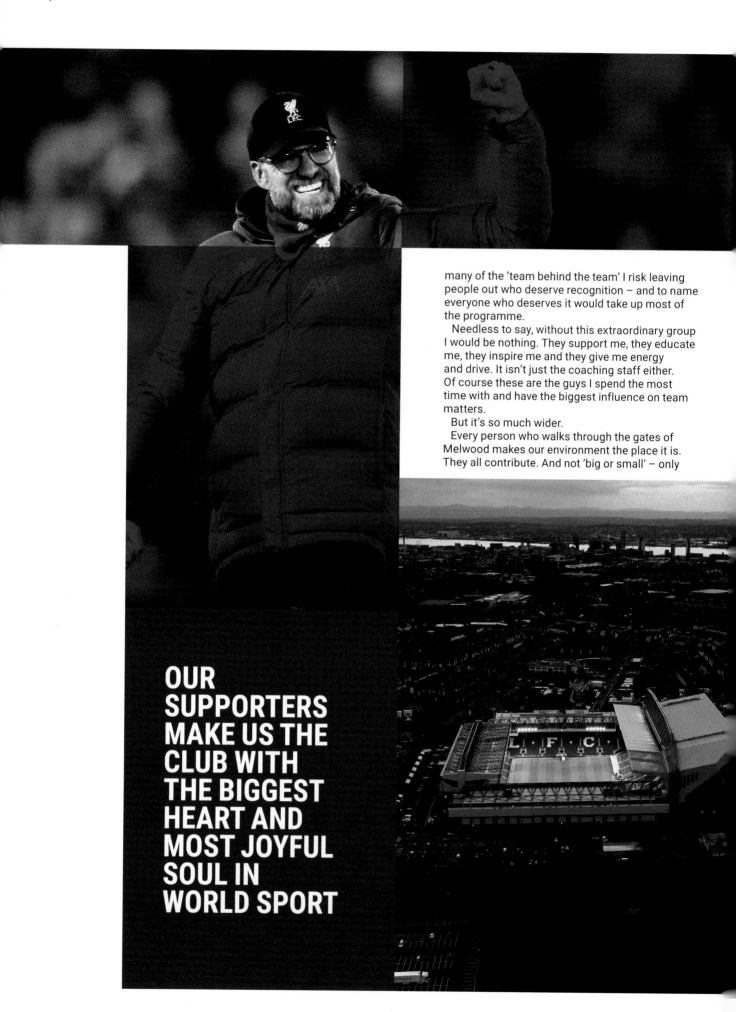

many of the 'team behind the team' I risk leaving people out who deserve recognition – and to name everyone who deserves it would take up most of the programme.

Needless to say, without this extraordinary group I would be nothing. They support me, they educate me, they inspire me and they give me energy and drive. It isn't just the coaching staff either. Of course these are the guys I spend the most time with and have the biggest influence on team matters.

But it's so much wider.

Every person who walks through the gates of Melwood makes our environment the place it is. They all contribute. And not 'big or small' – only

OUR SUPPORTERS MAKE US THE CLUB WITH THE BIGGEST HEART AND MOST JOYFUL SOUL IN WORLD SPORT

big, only important, only critical. They do the hard lifting in the shadows and allow the team and people like myself to enjoy the sunshine when times are good. But we know their value and they are as worthy of the title 'Champions' as anyone I can think of.

I did say it isn't right or possible to list names but there are two I simply must: Pepijn Lijnders and Peter Krawietz. Both are world-class coaches and leaders in their own right.

They have driven this team forward with their brains, knowledge and imagination. I could not be more appreciative of their contribution. I will forever be grateful.

Our supporters too, although absent since the season re-started, remain the wind in our sails. It is impossible to sum up their impact or their importance. They are the reason that representing this club brings the greatest possible emotional attachment and therefore emotional reward.

What we do here we do together. At times that has meant suffering together. But right now – and in the last 14 months – it has meant celebrating together. I love this.

It would not mean as much were it not for our supporters. They might not be in Anfield tonight in person but their spirit can be felt and we lift this trophy for them.

It has been their wait, their anguish, their dreams. I hope wherever in our city, region, the country or the world they watch from, they realise it is they that make LFC the club with the biggest heart and the most joyful soul in world sport.

Before moving to something more personal I must acknowledge our brilliant owners and football operations team. For FSG, unable to be here tonight because of the current global crisis, this title should act as vindication for smart and brave decisions made over the course of a decade.

Mike Gordon specifically. He is my friend as well as my 'boss'. He is the embodiment of the word 'supportive' - such a special guy – and he made this happen. He and John, Tom and FSG should be very proud tonight. And to Michael Edwards and his team likewise – incredibly smart people who have made nothing but outstanding decisions.

This is fulfilment of a vision.

And finally, for this season, this very

special campaign, I must say the words 'thank you' to the people who bring me the most joy of all. My family.

My wife Ulla who is my best friend on this planet. I love you so much. My two sons, Marc and Dennis, you have only ever brought me joy and a feeling of pride. What incredible men you have become. To see you grow as people beats any other achievement in life.

Doing this crazy job is fun because of these three people – my wife and my boys. The bad times are softened and the good times sweetened because we live through them together, as our own 'team'. They are my everything and my heart is constantly filled with love and happiness because of them.

I feel so blessed to have a situation where I am surrounded by people, personally and professionally, who make me realise what a wonderful gift life is.

The times we live in in this moment test us all. For some, the test is unfair and too much to bear. I know we are living through a period where for many joy must feel like a horizon you cannot reach or see. But I hope for the Liverpool family, what we have collectively experienced this season brings some warmth and comfort.

Tonight, when we end a 30-year wait, know that in that moment we will all experience something special and we will experience it together. If nothing else, this is the true beauty of our game and of this club. This is our moment. We have all earned it. So embrace it and cherish it.

Thank you.

You'll Never Walk Alone
Jürgen

Liverpool had waited a long, long time to lift the league title and Jürgen was delighted after leading the Reds to Premier League glory in 2019/20, a success celebrated in this winner's souvenir

'IT'S A WONDERFUL MOMENT'

JÜRGEN KLOPP

" I cannot sum up my emotions because if I tried to start talking about it [how I feel] again, I will start crying again! I am completely overwhelmed; I don't know, it's a mix of everything – I am relieved, I am happy, I am proud. I couldn't be more proud of the boys. How we watched the game [Chelsea v Manchester City] together, we knew it could happen, it could not happen, we didn't know.

"We want to play football and we are really happy that we are allowed to play again – then when it happened in that moment, it was a pure explosion. When we counted down the last five seconds of the game, the ref counted down a little bit longer than us so we had to look at two or three more passes! Then it was pure... I cannot describe it. It was a really, really nice moment. Directly after it, I felt so empty inside – I cannot believe it, I am really not happy with myself in the moment that I feel like I feel, but it's just a little bit too much in the moment. I will be fine, nobody has to worry!

"I actually couldn't be happier; I couldn't have dreamed of something like that and I never did before last year, honestly. We were not close enough three years ago, a year ago we were really close... what the boys have done in the last two-and-a-half years, the consistency they show is absolutely incredible and second to none. Honestly, I have no idea how we do that all the time. Last night, a very good example – we played a game [v Crystal Palace] like the stadium is fully packed and everybody is shouting 'Liverpool' or whatever constantly. It is a wonderful moment, that's what I can say.

"Thirty years ago... I was 23, so I didn't think too much about winning a title with Liverpool, to be honest! I had no skills for that! Thirty years later I am here and because of the great staff I have, it is unbelievable. It is for everybody; they all put so much effort into it and I am the lucky guy who sits in the seat in this moment and... can be part of this story. It's so great it is unbelievable.

"The boys love being part of this club, they love being part of the story of this club and the history. It is so nice how we learned how to deal with the history, how we learned to use the history in the last two years. It is just amazing."

2020/21

TESTING TIMES

Without question the trickiest season of Jürgen Klopp's Liverpool career and one of the most soulless in club history as the ongoing pandemic meant practically the entire campaign was played behind closed doors.

Losing centre-backs Virgil van Dijk, Joel Matip and Joe Gomez to season-ending injuries wrecked any realistic hopes of a title-defence despite the arrivals of Diogo Jota and Thiago Alcantara, and without their supporters behind them the Reds remarkably lost six consecutive home games at Anfield having also lost 7-2 at Aston Villa.

It was all put into perspective when Jürgen's mother Elisabeth passed away at the age of 81 and he was unable to return to Germany to attend her funeral.

The Reds began a new era off the pitch when moving from Melwood to the AXA Training Centre and on it a dramatic late winning goal by Alisson at West Bromwich Albion revitalised Klopp's injury-hit team. They rose from seventh to third to ensure Champions League qualification despite it being a season to forget.

LIVERPOOL FC
ISSUE 100

A milestone issue of the official club magazine featured the thoughts of the boss, from his next game mentality to not limiting yourself by targets, and which sporting star he thinks comes closest to aceing their talent...

NOBODY'S
PERFECT

What score would you give the manager out of 100?
Thought so. But, argues Jürgen Klopp, there is always –
always – room for improvement

79

Interview: UEFA.com

WE WANT TO TALK TO YOU ABOUT PERFECTION. WHAT DOES THE WORD MEAN TO YOU, BOTH IN LIFE AND IN SPORT, AND HOW WOULD YOU DEFINE IT?

Oh my God. That's what we have the ten minutes for, probably, to answer that question!

So. As a human, as a person, probably the first thing I realised that helped me a lot in life is that I don't have to go for perfection because it's not possible. I didn't even try, I just always tried to make the best of the things I had, and it never led anywhere close to perfection, to be honest. With football, it's pretty much the same.

So we are always trying to be as good as possible. But perfection, I never saw it, and I watch a lot of football as you

can imagine, and I never saw a perfect game. I saw perfect goals, perfect skills in a moment, but not a perfect game. But it's nice to try to go for it, because it keeps you going.

As long as you are not perfect, you have space to improve, which is nice and gives you the drive to get through all the different challenges you face during a football season, a football career, or life.

So I'm not a specialist in perfection, obviously. Probably the opposite, but I still try to push my boys to get there as close as possible.

BUT IF WE LOOK AT LIVERPOOL'S LEAGUE POSITIONS SINCE YOU TOOK OVER: EIGHTH, FOURTH, FOURTH, SECOND, AND FIRST. IT WAS A WORK-IN-PROGRESS AND NOW YOU'VE REACHED THE SUMMIT. HOW WOULD YOU COMPARE THE JOB OF MANAGING THE CLUB NOW TO WHEN YOU TOOK OVER?

It's obviously completely different because I know, now, everybody in the club, which was not the case when I came here. So you have an idea of what you want to do, but you have no real idea if you really can do it, because you have to know about all the people you work together with, and that's now.

My team is now my team, and not only the players. I mean the staff around as well. And I'm not the person who comes in and thinks: we have to change everything just because I'm here now.

In the beginning we didn't know a lot about each other, and obviously because of the history and tradition of English managers coming in and [having] a proper 'clean-out' in the training-ground, everybody was in doubt and thought I could sack them, because I think they were ninth or tenth in the table when I came here, and maybe the kitchen staff is responsible for that and that's why I'd clean out there as well. So they were not too sure what they can expect.

Now, we are completely different. We call ourselves a family and we are a family, and that's why I like the job today much more than I liked it when I came here.

DIOGO I LIKED, HONESTLY, FROM THE FIRST GAME I SAW HIM PLAYING FOR WOLVES... THE WAY HE PLAYED IN THE VERY INTENSE STYLE, THE ROLE HE HAD, THE DISCIPLINE HE SHOWED, PLUS THE CREATIVITY AND DESIRE...AND HIS SKILLS ARE PRETTY GOOD

WHEN THERE'S LESS ROOM FOR IMPROVEMENT, DOES THAT MEAN THE FRUIT IS HANGING HIGHER AND HIGHER?

What do you mean, 'less space for improvement'? I think there's a lot of space for improvement, maybe if you speak about the position in the table, yeah, there's not so much space, but for all the rest, oh my God. There's so much space for improvement. That's what we're working on.

But while you try to improve, you should never forget what is good already and use that, and that's what we do as well. So, it's not an obvious thing to do every morning: 'We have to get better, we have to get better'. No, we know some things are that good that it would sometimes be enough just to bring them consistently on the pitch.

WELL, MOST PEOPLE WOULD'VE SAID YOUR ATTACKING OPTIONS WERE PRETTY PERFECT. WHAT MADE YOU CONVINCED THAT DIOGO JOTA WOULD COME IN AND DO THE JOB HE HAS?

Actually I thought from something really good you never can have enough. I'm not sure about our options before and stuff like this. It's not about that. I was completely happy with all the squads I've had since I've been here but in the moment when you can change things, you should try to consider at least a change which could show up as an improvement.

And Diogo I liked, honestly, from the first game I saw him playing for Wolves. That's how it is. He had no idea about that, obviously, but for me it was always clear that when he

THIS IS NOT A SEASON OR A TIME IN LIFE WHEN YOU SHOULD LIMIT YOURSELF WITH TARGETS, IT'S JUST CONCENTRATE ON THE NEXT GAME, PLAY IT, CONCENTRATE AGAIN

was kind of in reach, I would go for him because [he's had a] very, very interesting and exciting career so far.

What he did, where he's come from, the moves he made, bam bam bam. And then the way he played for Wolves in the very, very intense style, the role he played, I liked the discipline he showed, plus the creativity he showed, plus the desire he showed.

And his skills are pretty good anyway, so I got a lot of good signs before we signed him that it could work out.

DO YOU HAVE TO BE QUITE CLINICAL IN THE TRANSFER-WINDOW BECAUSE YOU DIDN'T SIGN MANY?
We don't have a lot of space for failure, that's true. It's not that we buy a player for 50-odd million and then if it doesn't work out, we buy another one for 50 million, not for the same position.

For sure, things can always happen, that it doesn't work out and being unlucky with injuries is always bad. Nobody is really responsible for that. But it just takes, then, much longer to work out. But no, true, we have to be properly clinical.

YOUR START TO THE UEFA CHAMPIONS LEAGUE THIS YEAR WAS PERFECT, JUST THAT BLIP AGAINST ATALANTA BEFORE QUALIFICATION WAS SEALED…
Good!

EUROPEAN CHAMPIONS ARE ALWAYS REMEMBERED, BUT MULTIPLE CHAMPIONS HAVE A SPECIAL PLACE IN HISTORY. HOW DETERMINED ARE YOU TO HELP THE TEAM ACHIEVE THAT?
No, no, look. This is not a season, this is not a time in life when you should limit yourself, in a positive and a negative way, with targets. It's just we all have to get through this situation. That's how it is.

I think that's what we're all doing. Get through with [fewer] bruises, [fewer] knocks and stuff like this, or the lowest possible number, and then in the end if we get through the group stage, and we get through the last 16, eight, four, we will see what happens.

But it's not a target-directed season. I'm not sure if that's the right saying but the way you say: 'That's a target and if we don't reach it, we failed'. No, it's really just: 'Get through it'. Concentrate on the next game. Play it, and then either team will win it. Then concentrate on the next game, and that's how it works at the moment.

There's no moment where we think: oh, we probably can make it. I don't think there's any team in the world at the moment who can have the feeling that early anyway but also in general that 'We might be champions this year' in whichever competition, because nobody knows what happens.

For the players it's incredibly intense, what we are doing. We're all happy and it's without any alternative that we play. It's great, love it, fantastic, but it's all on the back of the players. They have to deliver. And honestly, you watch the game and you don't think about what they go through in the week, because we all have normal lives, obviously, left and right of the games we play.

And that's pretty much the same for all of us, where you cannot see friends, you cannot see your family, and all these things. And that's for…recovery, it's essential.

ROGER FEDERER VERY OFTEN LOOKS PERFECT… HE WOULD PROBABLY SAY NOT EVEN CLOSE, BUT I'VE SEEN GAMES OF HIS WHERE I THOUGHT YOU JUST CAN'T PLAY ANY BETTER

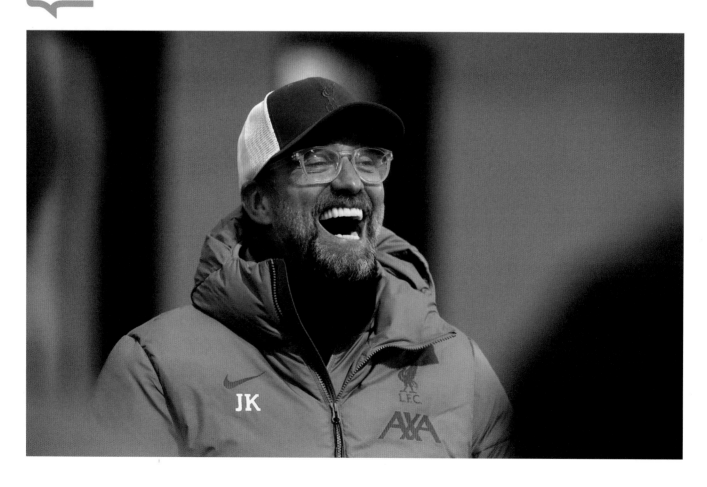

Recovery is not only sleep, it's not only treatment. It's really giving yourself a bit of freedom to think about things you want to think about and not what you have to think about. And that's obviously in the world out there at the moment, the biggest problem in that we don't have this time often enough and it keeps us quite tense.

That doesn't help if then you have every three days a game to play at 110 per cent, in the best way.

HOW DO YOU BECOME RELENTLESS OR ADAPT TO BEING RELENTLESS? ALSO, ONCE YOU'VE REACHED THE TARGET THAT WAS THE FOCUS, WHETHER THAT WAS CHAMPIONS OF EUROPE OR CHAMPIONS OF THE PREMIER LEAGUE...
Or of the world [laughs]. Sorry to mention it – it didn't happen that often in my life, so...

HOW DIFFICULT IS IT TO CHANGE THAT AND SAY OKAY, THE JOB'S DONE, FRESH TARGET, NEW SEASON, START AGAIN?
I don't know. I really don't know how it works. It's like you play a tennis game, you win it, and there's a next one. That's clear, that's the next game. You win it and it's the biggest thing in the world and it's the first time you've smashed Roger Federer, which will probably never happen. It will probably never happen, even when he's 56 or something.

But then there's the next one and you play it with all you have. And then there's a next one and you play it with all you have because you have no other chance to win this game. I think sports teach you that. It's clear, you win a game, great! Be happy, celebrate, perfect. But there's a next game.

So, what do you want to do with that? You go into the game and tell the other team: "By the way we won last week – what do you think about that?" They are not interested in it. They want to beat you with all you have. So, it's a completely natural process, for me, to stay greedy in sports. Not life but sports, 100 per cent.

That's because it's part of the game. You want to win. You play this game only for winning. We have fun, we love it, we really like what we do. But you could meet at a park with [smaller] challenges, honestly, and it's a nice game to play there, but we play against the best players in the world, so you want to win it.

LAST QUESTION: WHICH ATHLETE OR TEAM IN HISTORY DO YOU FEEL GOT CLOSE TO PERFECTION OR WERE PERFECT?
It's really interesting that I mentioned him a second ago, without knowing that the next question would be about that. But for me, very often, Roger Federer looks like...perfect. He will say, "Not even close", and yes, he lost games and stuff like this. But I saw games of him where I thought: I don't think you can play better.

But I'm not a specialist, obviously. I like tennis but other people know much more about it. There were moments when I thought: that's perfect. And it didn't happen a lot in other moments. So, yes, Roger.

2021/22

CUPS OF CHEER

Ibrahima Konate was Jürgen Klopp's sole summer signing before Luis Diaz was added to the ranks in January 2022, by which time his refreshed Reds were serious Premier League title contenders again.

Manchester United were thrashed 5-0 at Old Trafford and 4-0 at Anfield while home and away wins against Arsenal were amongst the highlights. After beating Chelsea on penalties in the Carabao Cup final at Wembley, Caoimhin Kelleher the hero, Liverpool remained in contention for an unprecedented quadruple and Klopp signed a contract extension.

A thrilling 3-2 FA Cup semi-final success against Manchester City was followed by another Wembley triumph against Chelsea on

penalties, Alisson Becker and Kostas Tsimikas the heroes, and Klopp's Redmen also reached the final of the Champions League, seeing off both Milan clubs, Benfica and Villarreal along the way.

With two games of the season to go the quadruple was still on, but despite losing only two Premier League games all season and beating Wolves on the final day, Manchester City's comeback win against Aston Villa was enough to pip the Reds to the title. There was also heartbreak in Paris when Real Madrid emerged triumphant with the only goal of the Champions League final, leaving Liverpool with two domestic cup wins to parade on the open-top bus.

By the time the Reds took on Villarreal in the semi-finals of the 2022 UEFA Champions League, a Beatles-inspired song in honour of the manager was proving to be a big hit on the Kop...

A SONG FOR EUROPE

The Merseybeat is back on the Spion Kop and this time it's manager Jürgen Klopp's turn to get the Fab Four treatment...you know, he said so

The words rang out from the Kop in the build-up to Roberto Firmino's second goal against SL Benfica a fortnight ago, a strike which all but booked Liverpool's passage into this semi-final. *"I'm so glad Jürgen is a Red, I'm so glad he delivered what he said"* The lyrics were from a new love song bestowed upon the boss as his team continued to make this season something out of the ordinary.

Sung to the Beatles track I Feel Fine, it's become a regular in recent weeks, resounding around Wembley in the FA Cup semi-final against Manchester City as well as the recent Premier League games against City, Manchester United and Everton. It's the latest in a series of tunes which have provided a soundtrack to Liverpool's recent successes in Europe and at home.

The single I Feel Fine originally reached the top of the UK charts on 12 December 1964 and remained there for five weeks. During that time the Reds – and they'd just begun to play in all-red – knocked out Anderlecht in the European Cup first round then won at West Bromwich Albion in the FA Cup third round. They'd reach the semi-finals of the former, losing to Inter Milan, and the final of the latter, beating Leeds United at Wembley to claim the trophy for the first time.

Back in the here-and-now and the quarter-final victory over Benfica earlier this month fired the Reds into their 12th European Cup/Champions League semi-final, a total that equals the English record.

Three of those semis have come under Klopp's leadership and over the next seven days he will be looking to guide Liverpool into a third Champions League final in five years.

The first, back in 2018, saw 'Allez Allez Allez', to the tune of L'estate Sta Finendo by Righeira, become the anthem for Liverpool's journey to Kyiv and the showpiece against Real Madrid.

As the Reds progressed through the rounds they did so to a tune that continues to ring out around Anfield today with scarves twirling. "We've conquered all of Europe, We're never gonna stop, From Paris down to Turkey..." And we all know the next line!

"Bob Paisley and Bill Shankly, The fields of Anfield Road, We are loyal supporters, And we come from Liverpool... ALLEZ ALLEZ ALLEZ!"

Local singer-songwriter and Liverpool fan Jamie Webster recorded a version which went down a storm, and twelve months later the Reds returned to the final and made amends for the heartbreak of the year before when they overcame Tottenham Hotspur 2-0 at the Wanda Metropolitano in Madrid.

One of the great sights of the build-up to the game in 2019 was Webster playing a set at the heaving fan-park at Plaza Felipe II with thousands of fans belting out the tunes.

Another unexpected side-effect of the 2018 defeat in Kyiv was an association between Liverpool FC and the singer

Dua Lipa after she had performed a mini-concert in the lead up to kick-off at the NSC Olimpiyskiy Stadium.

When the plans had been announced there was some scepticism considering the similarities to the use of pre-game entertainment in American sports. However, the 30,000 fans who had travelled 1,800 miles to Ukraine embraced the concept and despite the 3-1 defeat to Real Madrid, social-media clips of Reds singing One Kiss went viral.

"One of the highlights of the night was definitely seeing the video of all the Liverpool fans chanting along to One Kiss afterwards," Dua Lipa told the LFC website in 2020. "I felt very honoured."

The tune returned when Liverpool won their fifth major trophy under Klopp earlier this year following the Carabao Cup final triumph against Chelsea at Wembley. 'It lives on!' tweeted Dua Lipa as the red hordes at Wembley sang and danced at the end.

An honourable mention too for Gala's Freed from Desire, to which the players partied after they'd won the Premier League title in the summer of 2020.

Back to June 2019 when Liverpool beat Spurs in the Spanish capital in the final of Europe's premier club competition, and Klopp was interviewed post-match and famously said: "Let's talk about six, baby!" In the days and weeks that followed, supporters all over the world adopted the original Salt-N-Pepa hit from 1990 and tweaked it accordingly.

Klopp's very first season at Liverpool had also seen him take the club to a European final where they lost 3-1 to a Sevilla side managed by Unai Emery, the man who will be in the opposite technical area tonight.

The UEFA Europa League final was held in Basel that year and the afternoon leading up to the game was memorable for the sight of the travelling Kop belting out the words to Three Little Birds, the Bob Marley song adopted along the way.

The song came from the album Exodus, appropriately enough released in 1977, the year that Liverpool's love affair with the European Cup commenced with the capture of the trophy for the first time. "Don't worry, About a thing, Because every little thing, Is gonna be alright." With Klopp at the helm, fans knew these words would ring true.

The lyrics to the latest homage reference the biggest domestic prize rather than Europe: "Jürgen said to me you know, We'll win the Premier League you know, He said so – I'm in love with him and I feel fine." But on a night when 'The Yellow Submarine' is in town, what could be more appropriate?

All together now, *"I'm so glad..."*

WORDS: William Hughes

Carabao **ENERGY DRINK**

The boss enjoyed celebrating with the travelling Kop after a dramatic penalty shoot-out success over Chelsea sealed a record breaking ninth League Cup triumph

'After the game it was nice to celebrate with the people after a long time without having any reason to celebrate'

WORDS OF WEMBLEY WINNERS

JÜRGEN KLOPP

"We were here and lost a final in a penalty shootout like six, seven years ago. Afterwards nobody talks about it, it's like, 'You were twice at Wembley and you lost both finals'. It was a tight game, we were clearly better in the second half against Man City that time. We should have won it in the second half, didn't, and then in the shoot-out we lose. As a professional sportsperson, that's life. So now, in 10 years' time, nobody will ask, 'How did you win exactly against Chelsea?' You just have to win it. Were we better tonight than that time against City? I'm not 100 per cent sure, to be honest, but we are more experienced, that's a massive difference. We don't get nervous when things don't go well. We really keep our nerve.

"The start of the game was clearly better from Chelsea but all of a sudden, we were really in the game and then we let them run and we were the clear dominant team. I'm not sure 100 per cent but the first half was like 63 or something [per cent] possession – against Chelsea that's not that easy, so there was a lot of good football stuff obviously. But over 120 minutes you cannot hold them back and away from your goal, so they had their chances and obviously they scored 'goals' more than us, but they all were offside. That's pretty harsh to take for them I can imagine but I'm really happy about the effort and all these kind of things and yes, it's a big one for us because it's the first time for this group but the ninth time for the club, which is very important as well.

"Our fans were obviously quite happy about the whole thing tonight, the atmosphere was outstanding, I really loved it. And after the game it was nice to celebrate with the people after a long time without having any reason to celebrate something, or not the opportunity to celebrate something. So, I'm really happy about the whole thing.

"Facing Chelsea, there was like two lions going for each other – it was absolutely crazy. Then the penalty shoot-out, one of the most spectacular I ever saw. Absolutely great to win it like this. We called it the people's cup but the whole journey was a squad journey and that's what I love most about it."

In a May of mixed emotions, another breathless Wembley enounter with Chelsea saw the boss become only the second LFC manager to win all three domestic competitions after Sir Kenny Dalglish...

JÜRGEN SAID TO US, Y'KNOW...

The manager's post-match reaction at Wembley, and why he won't be telling Sadio where to place his penalties again any time soon!

After all that drama, the penalties and the pitchside media obligations, the two FA Cup final managers still had the small matter of their respective press conferences to fulfil, deep inside Wembley Stadium's labyrinthine layout, with it getting on for nine o'clock in the evening.

First to appear was Chelsea boss Thomas Tuchel, downbeat but commendably gracious as he fielded questions from the rows of journalists facing him. "No regrets," he said. "I told [my players] I was proud. We were competitive, we made life difficult for Liverpool. We played 240 minutes of final time [in the League Cup then FA Cup] and played a zero-zero against the most dangerous attacking team in the world. So we are sad but proud. That's life in sport. Everybody's in pain...

"I was impressed by both teams by the ability and quality to play a final. We've proved four times this season that we can produce peak performances to compete with them. The difference is they can do it Saturday-Wednesday-Saturday but we struggle. They can produce these type of performances more often. They've built this team over many years now – and this is the gap [between us and them]. They have an awful lot to play for. They are very consistent and we are the opposite.

"We did everything to win these matches, but Manchester City and Liverpool have proved you have to deliver on a consistent basis."

Fifteen minutes or so after Tuchel withdrew from the room, in came Klopp looking happy but a little drained, dressed in a bright red 'WINNERS' T-shirt with a medal around his neck. The opening question came from Sky Sports' Paul Gilmour, asking how best the boss could pay tribute to this group of players...

"YOU SAW WHAT IT MEANS"

"My team knows exactly what I think about them, that's the most important [thing]. This is again a trophy for the whole club – of course for the team, but for the whole club. We saw before the game already what it means to the people because our hotel is pretty central, we saw them all partying already since this morning. When we came into the stadium and looked at all the faces, like when we came to the bus, we could see what it means to the people. On the pitch with the performance you saw what it means to the players.

"It's unbelievable, it's massive, it's game number 60 or whatever in a very, very intense season, and putting out a performance like this is absolutely incredible. But most important – really most important – I have to say all respect to Chelsea. What a team, what a performance. In the end we all know a penalty shootout is a lottery. But we did it again. We work together with a company – four guys, their name is *neuro11*. I got in contact with them two years ago, I think, got aware of it. One of them is a neuroscientist and he said, 'We can train penalty-shooting'. 'Really?' I said, 'Sounds interesting, come over'. German guy, we met, we worked together and this trophy is for them obviously as well, like the Carabao Cup was.

"Sadio's penalty is for sure at least 50 per cent my responsibility because you have to let the boys do what they think they do, but with him I said, 'He knows you exactly, the goalie, so do the other way around'. How very often in my life, I realised it's better to shut up! But we still made it and honestly it means the world to us.

"It was difficult. The first 25 minutes were the best 25 minutes we played ever against Chelsea, we played an incredible game, but we didn't score. Then it's clear, Chelsea with the quality they have, they find a way back in the game. There were ups and downs in the game. They had their chances, we had massive chances, none of us used them. So a penalty shootout is a logical thing. Doing it like this feels good but gives you more a sense of how hard it must be for the opponent, because it would have been extremely hard for us in that moment after 120 minutes, losing like this. So, honestly, my respect to Chelsea and what they did."

"SO MANY SPECIAL STORIES"

"That we won now both domestic cups, that really is special. That Trent Alexander-Arnold is the youngest player ever in this incredible history of the Premier League who won all six major trophies, at 23, the youngest. So many special stories. And after the game I said to Thiago, 'If I would have known what a player you are, I would have signed you four years earlier'. He said, 'You taught me running!' I take that, it's fine. He could obviously already play football pretty well but he learned running in Liverpool, that's fine.

"So many special stories, Jordan Henderson obviously and these kinds of things. It's really cool. James Milner, at a quite advanced age having such an impact on a football team. Let me say, we had to change Mo early, which was not cool. It was my decision, it was pretty cautionary. Mo said, 'I feel something, [but] I can carry on'. I said, 'No'. A football game is not a perfect physiotherapist, it means it rarely gets better during a game. Then Virg stands with me and says, 'I feel something but it's fine I think'. We make a decision together, so he stays on but was clear when we didn't make it in 90 minutes he has to go off. Then you can bring Diogo Jota and Joel Matip in this moment – that's the best situation I've ever been in as a coach, to be honest. That's absolutely outstanding, that's why we had the chance to go for it.

"It was difficult, we know that. It was lucky, we know that. But we deserved it as well and that's really cool."

"IT FEELS MASSIVE"

"The best physiotherapist is winning football games, to be honest. Robbo had a cramp, so that's obviously normal and completely fine. I was surprised that more players didn't have cramp, to be honest, after what we had to do tonight. So before you are in a situation, you never know exactly how big it feels. It feels massive. I cannot believe it. It feels massive. The only problem I have is that we cannot

really celebrate it because we play on Tuesday. I think: how can you do that? It's such a fantastic competition, such a fantastic occasion and then you limit the celebration – okay, obviously not for the people, they can do what they want – but for the team by putting in a game on Tuesday. It is like it is and from here we go."

"VAMOS!"

"What a boy, what a story, what a player [Luis Diaz is] – but he should have scored! I think we agree. He agrees probably. So the speed he has is insane. Not to forget, he played on the side of Chalobah and Reece James and getting in a situation like this is absolutely unlikely. The big chance he had in the first half, I think it was a pass from Trent – if you want, we can talk about *his* performance as well, by the way – and he should have scored in that moment with his quality. That's how it is. But what a player. He's outstanding. He's a fantastic boy. It's so funny, so we hug each other after the game and just shout 'Vamos!' and whatever, the few words I know in a similar language. But he gets our football 100 per cent. We thought we saw that at Porto but that it's really like this, I feel really lucky as well, to be honest. He fits like a glove to our football and that's really, really special."

"WE DON'T STOP HERE"

"I don't have to make this decision [about where this team ranks among the greatest ever] and I don't have to judge this and have to think about that. Other people have to do that. I couldn't care less, to be honest. I enjoy the moment with these boys. We are so incredibly close with each other and with our fans – it's a pure joy to be part of this club in the moment. There's a lot to come and a lot to play for, we all know that. But for tonight I decided to take that and just enjoy this moment and don't think about the next challenge we are facing. Because it's really special, it's really special.

"Imagine, like 20 years ahead and then you look back... Jordan Henderson is probably then a pundit or maybe not even a pundit anymore because he thought that makes no sense anymore, so in 20 years then you think: he's the captain of the only Liverpool team so far – hopefully not the only because maybe we can do it again, which will be completely ridiculous – but he was the first captain who won four trophies, as an example. The Trent story. All these other stories. Where Virgil van Dijk was six years ago in his career when he thought: where will it go? When we go five years back, Ibou Konate probably played in the under-16s of whatever team in France. And now we are here for this moment.

"We don't finish, it's just now for the moment a little reflection. But we don't have to decide where this team ranks. I know a few players of these teams but I cannot say how they played. But I'm pretty sure in the time when they played, they were the best teams. But meanwhile, we know so much more about training, we know so much more about sports science, all these kind of things. That's why these boys are obviously much fitter than the former generations were – it's nothing to do with football talent or whatever. If the players from the past, like Rushie or Kenny, if they would've been trained like the boys are trained today, imagine that? That would be crazy. So, it's all good for the moment. We don't stop here, we just take the time to enjoy it for a few minutes.

"We came from a season last year where nobody thought, I'm 100 per cent sure in this room nobody thought, apart from me maybe, that we can go again like we did this year. That we could do it is all because of the character of these players – it's the only reason. Because I can say whatever I want, I can motivate as much as I want, [but] if these boys don't listen, if these boys are a little bit distracted by whatever or get weak or soft or whatever, then in this moment you don't have a chance...

"But today is FA Cup and we won the game and we have the medal, a wonderful T-shirt. That's enough for the moment."

2022/23

HIGHS AND LOWS

New signing Darwin Nunez announced himself to Liverpool supporters when scoring on his debut as Jürgen Klopp lifted a seventh different piece of silverware in the shape of the FA Community Shield, but the summer departure of Sadio Mane seemed to set the Reds back.

A Premier League record-equalling 9-0 win against Bournemouth and club record 7-0 hammering of Manchester United were among the highlights at Anfield while Mo Salah scored the quickest hat-trick in Champions League history during a 7-1 victory at Rangers, but

Klopp's side were hit by injuries again and lacked consistency.

Knocked out of the League Cup at Man City and the FA Cup at Brighton, home and away reverses to Real Madrid ended Liverpool's Champions League campaign despite the January recruitment of Cody Gakpo.

The Reds rallied in the run-in and won seven games on the bounce including 6-1 at Leeds, but had left themselves with too much to do and finished fifth, ending a six-season stint in the Champions League in which Klopp had taken Liverpool to three finals.

In his programme notes for the final game of the 2022/23 campaign, Jürgen paid tribute to four fine servants of the club who were moving on to pastures new after playng a big part in recent successes

Good afternoon and welcome to Anfield for our final home Premier League game of the season against Aston Villa. This will be a special occasion for many reasons. Every game we play at this stadium is 'special' but today is extra because this will be our chance to bid farewell to a group of players who between them have made an incredible contribution to our club during a period which I think everyone will agree has not been too bad.

For Roberto Firmino, Naby Keita, James Milner and Alex Oxlade-Chamberlain I have nothing but the very best wishes. If we had the space, I could take page after page listing the moments that they gave us, the qualities that they brought and the collective that they have been part of. But the best way of measuring the contribution is much more straightforward because it can be found in the respect that they have earned from their team-mates, staff and our supporters.

The medals that they will leave with say everything that you could possibly need to know about what they have achieved during their time here, but on top of that there are the memories and the experiences which we have shared. In this respect it seems to me that we were definitely blessed to have them and I would hope that they also feel blessed to have been with us.

I would also like to wish Arthur Melo well as his loan period comes to an end. Circumstances meant Arthur was not able to play as much as he would have liked but his professionalism and ability were clear to all who worked with him.

One of my favourite moments of the season came on Monday night with the away fans who travelled to Leicester showing Bobby how much they love him by

FROM THE BOSS

JÜRGEN KLOPP

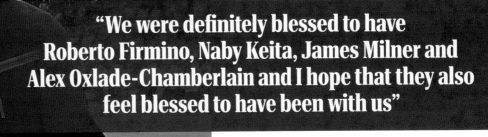

"We were definitely blessed to have Roberto Firmino, Naby Keita, James Milner and Alex Oxlade-Chamberlain and I hope that they also feel blessed to have been with us"

be and I have said many times that I do not expect them to fall away, but I also know from past experience that if I was them I would not want any of the teams below to keep on winning.

So this is our objective and it makes sense for it to be this way not only because it keeps possibilities open. It also makes sense because what we do now in terms of the football we play, the results we get and the momentum we can build can only help us going forward. This season might end next week but our ambitions do not and the best thing about one campaign finishing is that it will not be too long before another one begins.

The problem today is that we have an opponent in Aston Villa who are also in very, very good form. I think I am right in saying that their results in the second half of this season have been the second-best in the league which tells us everything that we could know about their quality and also the challenge that they will bring.

Unai Emery is a manager who I have come across quite a few times in my career and it will not surprise anyone who knows his work that Villa are doing as well as they are. I am sure that he would recognise the strength of the squad that he inherited from Steven Gerrard and the work that he did at Villa, but Unai's own efforts speak for themselves and I could not be more respectful of the work that he is doing.

Finally – and this is definitely a case of last but not least – I would like to take this opportunity to thank our fans for the support that you have given us this season. It would be fair to say that you could have asked for more from us and also that we will be asking more of ourselves going forward, but we could not have asked for more from you.

From the first day of the season, home and away and in good times and bad, your backing has been incredible and I could not be more grateful.

Hopefully we can enjoy today together in all the respects that we would want.

singing his name non-stop for so long that the only way it could have been brought to an end was by Trent scoring a world-class goal. I hope today all four of our departees will feel the same kind of affection from all of us because that is what they deserve.

Of course, the priority today is to perform as well as we can and to do everything in our power to pick up another three points as we look to continue our strong ending to a tough season.

There is no need for us to talk about targets at this stage – our main responsibility is simply to maintain the standards of recent weeks and to see where that might take us.

It has already taken us to a Europa League place which did not seem possible a couple of months ago and after this we will see what happens. The clubs who are above us in the league table are there because they deserve to

You'll Never Walk Alone
Jürgen

2023/24

LIVERPOOL 2.0

The shock departure of skipper Jordan Henderson and Fabinho, on the back of James Milner, Roberto Firmino, Naby Keita and Alex Oxlade-Chamberlain all leaving, meant it was time for a midfield reset as Jürgen Klopp built his 'Liverpool 2.0'.

A whole new midfield of Alexis Mac Allister, Dominik Szoboszlai, Wataru Endo and Ryan Gravenberch were recruited and Klopp put his faith in the Academy as young players such as Conor Bradley, Jarell Quansah, Bobby Clark, James McConnell, Jayden Danns and Lewis Koumas were given opportunities alongside Curtis Jones and Harvey Elliott when senior stars were missing through injury.

Reenergised, Liverpool became embroiled in a three-way Premier League title fight with Arsenal and Manchester City, beat Chelsea 1-0 in the 'Klopp's Kop Kids' Carabao Cup final thanks to an extra-time header by Virgil van Dijk and progressed to the quarter-final of the Europa League.

Yet there had also been an enormous shock when Jürgen Klopp announced on 26 January 2024 that he was running out of energy and this would be his last campaign as LFC manager.

He leaves with a win percentage of over 60% from his 491 games in charge and Liverpool FC simply won't be the same without him.

Jürgen won his seventh major trophy at LFC when 'Klopp's Kids' helped deliver the League Cup on a memorable afternoon at Anfield South

THE MANAGER SPEAKS...

JÜRGEN KLOPP

"What we saw here today is so exceptional. We might never see it again and not because I am on the sideline, but because these things don't happen in football. I got told outside that there's an English phrase, 'You don't win trophies with kids' – I didn't know that. Yeah?! There are longer careers than mine but in more than 20 years, [it's] easily the most special trophy I ever won. It's absolutely exceptional. Sometimes I get asked if I'm proud of this, proud of that, proud of that, and it's really tricky. I wish I could feel pride more often, I just don't. Tonight though, there's an overwhelming feeling, 'Oh my God, what's going on here?' I was proud of everybody involved in everything here.

I was proud of our people for the way they pushed us. I was proud of the staff for creating this kind of atmosphere surrounding where these boys can just do what they are best at. I was proud of our Academy. I was proud of my coaches.

I was proud of so many things. It was really overwhelming. It had nothing to do with maybe my last game at Wembley – I checked that, nothing to do with that. It was really because of how everybody contributed, seeing the faces after the game of the kids – Jayden Danns. Can you create in football stories which definitely nobody will ever forget? It's so difficult because this happened before, this happened before, they won it then, there. If you find the same story with academy players coming on against a top, top, top side and still winning it, I never heard it.

"This was so special. You saw the game, you saw the circumstances. We had problems before the game, they became bigger during the game... And then getting through all of this, you see tired players. For tonight it is a night I will never forget. If nobody else sees it like that, no problem. For me, it's a really nice memory, forever."

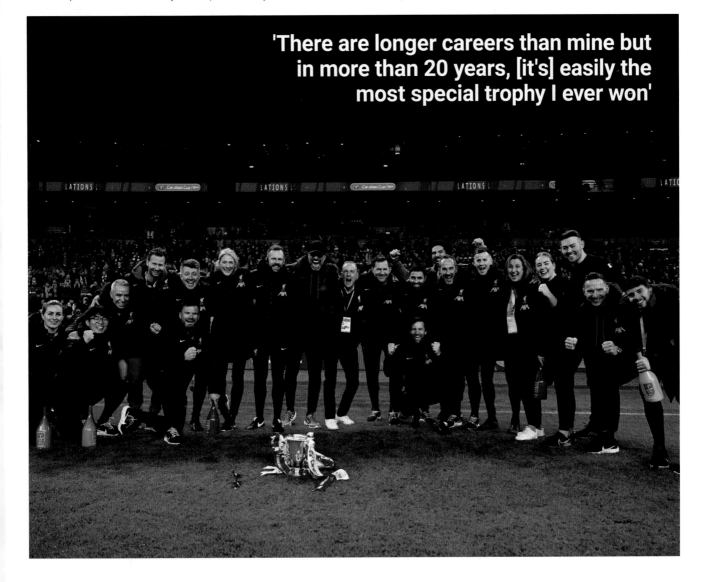

'There are longer careers than mine but in more than 20 years, [it's] easily the most special trophy I ever won'

101

The various pieces of spectacular street art around Liverpool produced in honour of Jürgen Klopp were among the subjects featured in the official club book The Art of LFC which was published in 2023...

It started with a Klopp

The man who brought back the good times for Liverpool FC has tributes in town and in Anfield ⊙

Liverpool were winning 4-0 away to Bournemouth in the Premier League when something positively seminal happened back in the city's Baltic neighbourhood. It was December 2018 and while Mohamed Salah was firing the Reds to the top of the table with a hat-trick down on the South Coast, graffiti artist Akse was putting Jürgen Klopp for posterity upon a wall on Jordan Street over the course of the same weekend.

Akse's previous subjects had included Muhammad Ali, David Bowie and Stephen Hawking. The Baltic meanwhile was a vibrant area already famous for its street-art as well as its football screenings, making it the ideal location for the mural. Klopp himself, instantly recognisable with that infectious smile and once described by the club's former chief-executive Peter Moore as "one of the more holistic human beings you will ever meet," was the perfect subject.

The following August another depiction of the Reds boss appeared on the wall of an Anfield bar, Klopp's Boot Room on Houlding Street. It was created by street-artist John Culshaw who described the commission as "a pleasure to work on because I am a huge LFC fan. I would say he is our best manager since Bill Shankly and this mural is a personal tribute to him from me.

"It was at the beginning of the season where we won the league," he told the club's website. "Everyone just had this feeling that we were going to do it that year, so I thought: I want to go and paint Jürgen Klopp somewhere. I got in touch with a few mates who are in Liverpool fan-groups and said, 'Can anyone get me a wall?' One got back to me saying his friend had a little matchday hotel called Klopp's Boot Room, right opposite The Sandon, and they said I could use it.

"They thought I was going to do a little something, but when I got there I said to him, 'Do you mind if I board your windows up?' And he went, 'Why – how big is it going to be?' I said, 'As big as I can, basically!' So I boarded the windows up and stuck a massive Klopp piece on the side, and it came out well."

Three years later in September 2022 a third Jürgen tribute appeared, close to the stadium and covering a whole end-terrace in Randolph Street. The work of another street-artist, Hugh Whitaker, and a collaboration between MurWalls and BOSS Night, it took four days to create and

Right and above: the Randolph Street tribute to Jürgen at Anfield
Opposite: John Culshaw's Klopp mural outside a bar near the stadium

featured a line from the *I Feel Fine* song reworked by the Kop in honour of the manager.

Daniel Nicolson, on behalf of BOSS Night, told the club's website: "It's been fantastic to see the streets around the ground decorated over the past couple of years with murals, but we felt there was one person absent: Jürgen. While there is a superb Klopp painting in the Baltic, the man who has brought us so much joy over the past seven years was missing from L4.

"All of us at BOSS feel a connection on and off the pitch to Jürgen. He's been to our events, he speaks highly of [musician] Jamie Webster, we know he enjoys watching all the videos from gigs. And, of course, for the wider fanbase as a whole he is revered. So we wanted to show appreciation to him on behalf of all Reds around the world.

"The support for it has been unbelievable. Chatting to the locals, I know how much this means to them – the football club is a big part of the community. What Jürgen has done for them, it's a very proud moment for me to do this."

Two months later, Klopp was officially awarded the Freedom of the City of Liverpool at a ceremony held in the Town Hall, in acknowledgement of his achievements since arriving at LFC in 2015. In that time he'd overseen seven trophy successes, including of course the Champions League 2019 and the Premier League in 2020 to end the club's three-decade wait to win the top-flight title again.

But, as Daniel Nicolson and Peter Moore both touched upon, there is more to Jürgen Klopp than winning silverware, not least the way he has orchestrated a communion with loud, colourful, youthful LFC fan culture. "It's not 'glory hunting', it's 'journey hunting'," he once wrote in his matchday programme column.

Don't mention that *I Feel Fine* tune, though. "I still struggle that it's for me. I am every day in front of a camera so I'm obviously not shy...but I am not the main man. The players play, and [even though] you sing all the time my name, I don't play. But I love the song, I'm very, very, very thankful for the idea."

Not nearly as much as the rest of us, boss.

JÜRGEN KLOPP

PLAYER APPEARANCES FOR LIVERPOOL UNDER JÜRGEN KLOPP

(all competitions - as at 14/04/24)

Player	Apps	Player	Apps
ROBERTO FIRMINO	355	MARKO GRUJIC	16
MOHAMED SALAH	342	BOBBY CLARK	14
JAMES MILNER	323	OZAN KABAK	13
JORDAN HENDERSON	304	SHEYI OJO	13
TRENT ALEXANDER-ARNOLD	303	PEDRO CHIRIVELLA	11
ANDY ROBERTSON	291	BEN WOODBURN	11
SADIO MANE	269	BEN DOAK	10
VIRGIL VAN DIJK	263	BRAD SMITH	10
ALISSON	256	JON FLANAGAN	9
GEORGINIO WIJNALDUM	237	JAMES McCONNELL	9
FABINHO	219	TYLER MORTON	9
JOE GOMEZ	218	CAMERON BRANNAGAN	8
JOEL MATIP	201	OVIE EJARIA	8
DIVOCK ORIGI	171	CONNOR RANDALL	8
ALEX OXLADE-CHAMBERLAIN	146	KAIDE GORDON	7
DIOGO JOTA	143	JOAO TEIXEIRA	7
DEJAN LOVREN	141	ADAM BOGDAN	5
ADAM LALLANA	130	RHIAN BREWSTER	4
CURTIS JONES	129	LUKE CHAMBERS	4
NABY KEITA	129	STEVEN CAULKER	4
EMRE CAN	116	JAYDEN DANNS	4
HARVEY ELLIOTT	112	KI-JANA HOEVER	4
SIMON MIGNOLET	100	SEPP VAN DEN BERG	4
THIAGO	98	OWEN BECK	3
NATHANIEL CLYNE	93	LEIGHTON CLARKSON	3
LUIS DIAZ	91	ELIJAH DIXON-BONNER	3
ALBERTO MORENO	90	JOSE ENRIQUE	3
DANIEL STURRIDGE	90	TIAGO ILORI	3
PHILIPPE COUTINHO	89	DANNY WARD	3
DARWIN NUNEZ	89	MORGAN BOYES	2
IBRAHIMA KONATE	87	RAFA CAMACHO	2
KOSTAS TSIMIKAS	85	MELKAMU FRAUENDORF	2
CODY GAKPO	73	HERBIE KANE	2
LUCAS	65	BILLY KOUMETIO	2
XHERDAN SHAQIRI	63	YASSER LAROUCI	2
TAKUMI MINAMINO	55	JAMES NORRIS	2
RAGNAR KLAVAN	53	CALVIN RAMSAY	2
LORIS KARIUS	49	CALUM SCANLON	2
CAOIMHIN KELLEHER	47	JEROME SINCLAIR	2
ALEXIS MAC ALLISTER	39	HARRY WILSON	2
DOMINIK SZOBOSZLAI	38	MAX WOLTMAN	2
WATARU ENDO	37	ARTHUR	1
CHRISTIAN BENTEKE	36	JACK BEARNE	1
JOE ALLEN	33	HARVEY BLAIR	1
RYAN GRAVENBERCH	33	JAKE CAIN	1
JORDON IBE	33	SERGI CANOS	1
NECO WILLIAMS	33	ISAAC CHRISTIE-DAVIES	1
NATHANIEL PHILLIPS	29	TONY GALLACHER	1
MAMADOU SAKHO	29	JOE HARDY	1
JARELL QUANSAH	28	TOM HILL	1
CONOR BRADLEY	27	RYAN KENT	1
DOMINIC SOLANKE	27	LEWIS KOUMAS	1
ADRIAN	26	ADAM LEWIS	1
KOLO TOURE	24	LUIS LONGSTAFF	1
STEFAN BAJCETIC	21	JOE MAGUIRE	1
FABIO CARVALHO	21	LIAM MILLAR	1
KEVIN STEWART	20	MATEUSZ MUSIALOWSKI	1
RHYS WILLIAMS	19	TREY NYONI	1
MARTIN SKRTEL	18	JORDAN ROSSITER	1
DANNY INGS	17	LAYTON STEWART	1

VIRGIL VAN DIJK	23	NATHANIEL CLYNE	2
GEORGINIO WIJNALDUM	22	JAYDEN DANNS	2
CODY GAKPO	21	WATARU ENDO	2
TRENT ALEXANDER-ARNOLD	18	RAGNAR KLAVAN	2
ALEX OXLADE-CHAMBERLAIN	18	MAMADOU SAKHO	2
CURTIS JONES	16	ALISSON	1
ADAM LALLANA	14	STEFAN BAJCETIC	1
TAKUMI MINAMINO	14	CONOR BRADLEY	1
EMRE CAN	13	BOBBY CLARK	1
JORDAN HENDERSON	13	KAIDE GORDON	1
FABINHO	11	MARKO GRUJIC	1
NABY KEITA	11	KI-JANA HOEVER	1
JOEL MATIP	11	DANNY INGS	1
HARVEY ELLIOTT	9	LEWIS KOUMAS	1
ANDY ROBERTSON	9	LUCAS	1
CHRISTIAN BENTEKE	8	ALBERTO MORENO	1
XHERDAN SHAQIRI	8	SHEYI OJO	1
DEJAN LOVREN	7	NATHANIEL PHILLIPS	1
DOMINIK SZOBOSZLAI	7	JARELL QUANSAH	1
ALEXIS MAC ALLISTER	6	JEROME SINCLAIR	1
JORDON IBE	4	MARTIN SKRTEL	1
JOE ALLEN	3	BRAD SMITH	1
FABIO CARVALHO	3	DOMINIC SOLANKE	1
RYAN GRAVENBERCH	3	JOAO TEIXEIRA	1
IBRAHIMA KONATE	3	KOLO TOURE	1
THIAGO	3	BEN WOODBURN	1

109

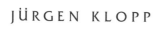

Stats supplied by Ged Rea and Dave Ball

JÜRGEN KLOPP:
HIS LIVERPOOL CAREER

The only member of the current squad that Jürgen Klopp inherited in October 2015 is Joe Gomez.

Jürgen has given first team debuts to 90 players during his time at Anfield – the first being Connor Randall in October 2015; the last Mateusz Musialowski in March 2024.

In January 2024 Liverpool defeated Chelsea 4-1 to give Klopp his 200th league win as Reds manager. He achieved the landmark in fewer games than any boss in history, just 318 matches, 37 fewer than Bob Paisley.

In March 2024 Klopp became only the third Reds manager to see his team score 1,000 goals during his tenure, following Bill Shankly (1959-74) - 1,307 goals in 783 games and Tom Watson (1896-1915) - 1,226 goals in 742 games. His figures are 1,020 goals in 484 games (2015-14 April 2024).

Jürgen has the highest percentage win ratio in league games of any Liverpool manager who has been in charge for more than 30 matches. It currently stands at 62.19%.

Klopp has used 120 different players in all competitions from a total of 33 nations.

The players who have made the most appearances are Roberto Firmino (355) and Mo Salah (342).

He has chosen 23 different captains in all his games in charge – Jordan Henderson wore the armband on most occasions (247).

Six of the Reds' seven youngest FA Cup scorers have all found the net during the time of Jürgen Klopp.

The seven youngest starting XIs ever selected by the club have all been on Jürgen's watch. The youngest average was for the FA Cup tie with Shrewsbury Town in February 2020 at just 19 years and 102 days.

Jürgen has been responsible for three of Liverpool's four highest ever league points totals, which includes the record tally of 99, accrued in 2019/20. Adjusting to three points for a win, the second highest came under Bob Paisley in 1978/79 with 98.

He has overseen Liverpool's record number of away wins in a league campaign – the 14 they won in 2019/20.

Jürgen was awarded back-to-back FIFA Coach of the Year awards in 2019 and 2020.

The first goal scored under Jürgen was recorded by Emre Can in a 1-1 home draw with Rubin Kazan in the Europa League in Klopp's second match in charge.

His first victory as Liverpool manager came in October 2015 when Nathaniel Clyne's goal gave them a 1-0 League Cup win over Bournemouth at Anfield.

In December 2019 against Everton, Liverpool set a new club record of 32 top-flight league games without defeat – a run they extended to 44.

In February 2020 Klopp's side equalled the English top-flight record for most consecutive wins (18) and later in that season set a top-flight record of 24 successive home league victories.

In November 2020, Klopp led Liverpool to a club record 64th consecutive league match unbeaten at Anfield. The run eventually ended at 68.

Klopp has twice been voted LMA Manager of the Year and Premier League Manager of the Season – in the same seasons of 2019/20 and 2021/22.

He has been voted Premier League Manager of the Month on 10 occasions.

In 2022 Klopp was awarded the Freedom of the City of Liverpool, becoming only the second foreign national to be given the honour after Nelson Mandela.

Jürgen has faced 75 different opponents during his time at Anfield. He has failed to defeat only Real Madrid, Sion and Sevilla.

62 different players have scored for Liverpool during Jürgen's tenure with Mo Salah topping the list – his current tally is 209.

The man who has played more Premier League minutes under Jürgen Klopp is Mo Salah with 20,029.

Jürgen has used 57 different centre-back partnerships in his time with the most popular permutation being Joel Matip/Virgil van Dijk – 93 times.

In the FA Cup tie at Manchester United in March, Wataru Endo became the 97th player to be used by Jürgen in the competition.

Nine times a Liverpool substitute has scored within a minute of coming on to the pitch in a Premier League fixture. Five of those have come with Jürgen Klopp as a manager – two from Daniel Sturridge and one each from Divock Origi, James Milner and Takumi Minamino.

In European competition he has had more games as Liverpool boss against Spanish opposition than against any other nation – 19. The games against Atalanta in April brought the number of meetings with Italian clubs to 16.

The Reds' fastest ever Premier League goal came under Jürgen – Naby Keita scoring after 15 seconds against Huddersfield Town at Anfield in April 2019.

Liverpool have started more than twice as many games under Jürgen at 8pm (119) than they have at the traditional time of 3pm (56).

In the reign of the man from Stuttgart, Liverpool have played in 11 penalty shoot-outs, winning seven.

Appointed on 8 October 2015, Klopp has won the Champions League, UEFA Super Cup, FIFA World Club Cup, Premier League, League Cup (twice) and FA Cup and is the only Liverpool manager to win six different major trophies.

Only once has Jürgen been forced to make a goalkeeper-for-goalkeeper substitution while at Liverpool. Adrian came on for Alisson in the home victory over Norwich City in August 2019.

Liverpool Football Club's two longest runs of successive league victories have come under Jürgen – 18 from October 2019-February 2020 and 17 from March-October 2019.

The Reds have been involved in eight European group stages with Jürgen in charge, including the majority of the 2015/16 Europa League campaign. They finished on top six times and second on the other two occasions.

Under Jürgen Klopp, Liverpool have scored 17 winning goals from the 90th minute onwards in the Premier League. Sadio Mane, Divock Origi and Darwin Nunez have each done so twice.

The 2019/20 league title success was achieved with more games to spare than any other title victory in English top-flight history. They won it with seven games to play.

The highest number of goals Liverpool have scored at Anfield in a Premier League campaign is the 55 scored in 2018/19.

Liverpool won 32 times during the 2019/20 Premier League season – the most they have ever accrued in a single league campaign.

In 2019 Liverpool won 83.79% of all their league fixtures – the highest percentage rate in any calendar year in their history.

Jürgen gave 23 players a Liverpool debut in all competitions in 2019/20 – the most of any season in the club's existence.

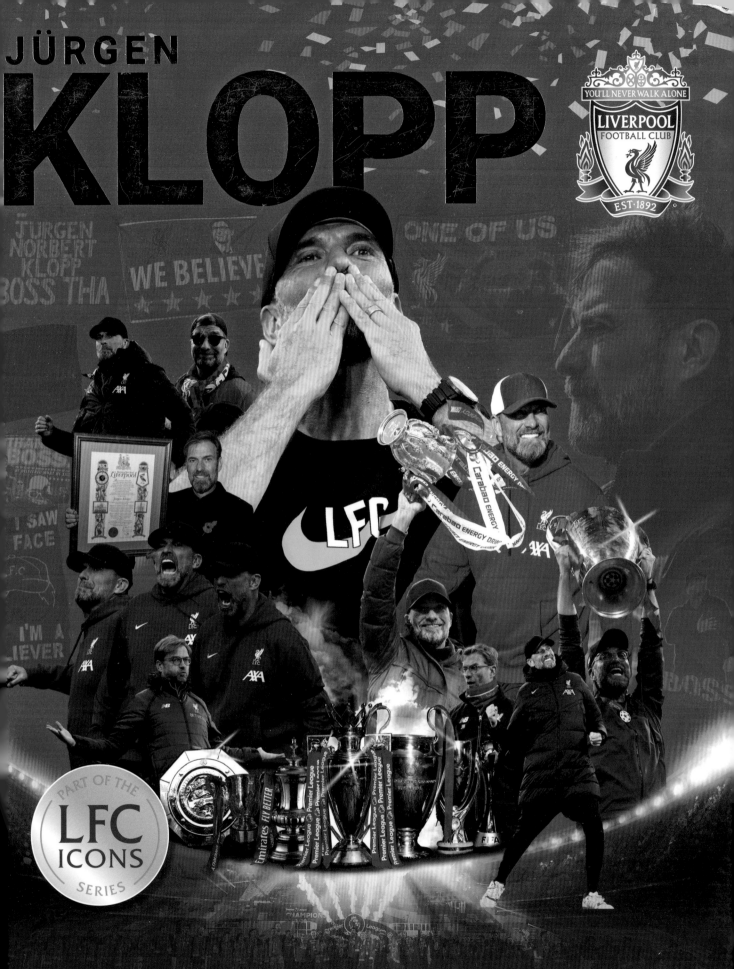

JÜRGEN KLOPP

I'M SO GLAD THAT JÜRGEN IS A RED

OFFICIAL LIVERPOOL FOOTBALL CLUB SPECIAL SOUVENIR

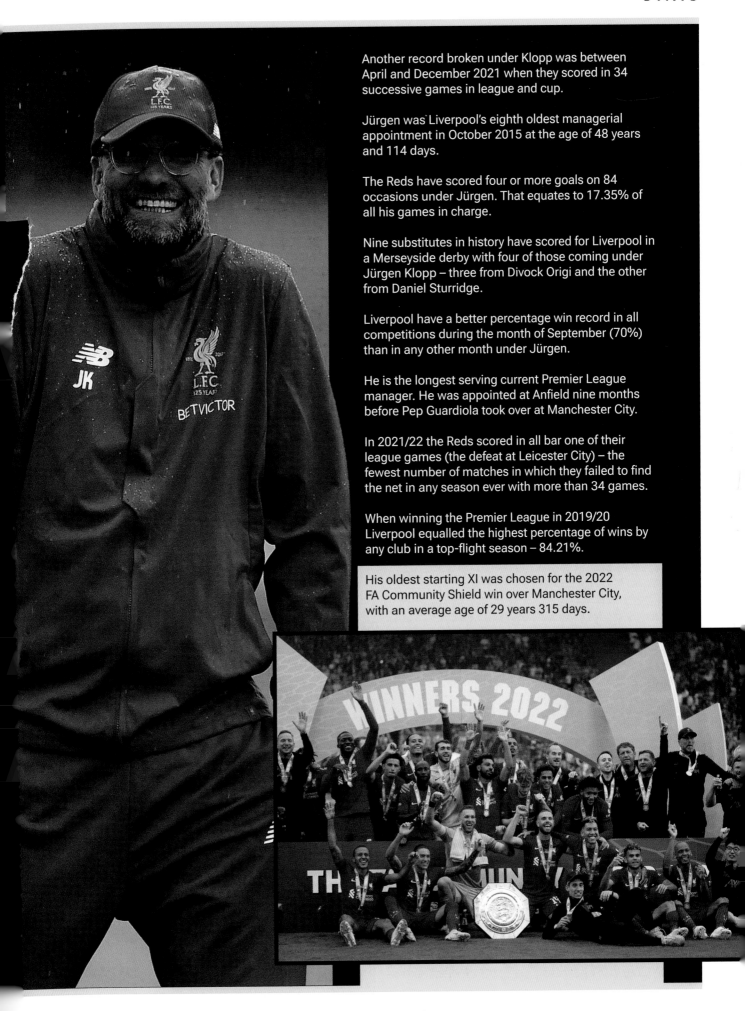

Another record broken under Klopp was between April and December 2021 when they scored in 34 successive games in league and cup.

Jürgen was Liverpool's eighth oldest managerial appointment in October 2015 at the age of 48 years and 114 days.

The Reds have scored four or more goals on 84 occasions under Jürgen. That equates to 17.35% of all his games in charge.

Nine substitutes in history have scored for Liverpool in a Merseyside derby with four of those coming under Jürgen Klopp – three from Divock Origi and the other from Daniel Sturridge.

Liverpool have a better percentage win record in all competitions during the month of September (70%) than in any other month under Jürgen.

He is the longest serving current Premier League manager. He was appointed at Anfield nine months before Pep Guardiola took over at Manchester City.

In 2021/22 the Reds scored in all bar one of their league games (the defeat at Leicester City) – the fewest number of matches in which they failed to find the net in any season ever with more than 34 games.

When winning the Premier League in 2019/20 Liverpool equalled the highest percentage of wins by any club in a top-flight season – 84.21%.

His oldest starting XI was chosen for the 2022 FA Community Shield win over Manchester City, with an average age of 29 years 315 days.

The Reds have topped 100 goals scored in five of his seven full seasons so far and are well over a ton of goals this season, too.

The 1,020 goals Liverpool have currently scored under Klopp have come at an average of 2.11 per game.

Under Jürgen's management, Liverpool's most frequently occurring result is a 2-0 victory, which has happened 51 times closely followed by 49 wins of 2-1.

The Reds' 1,000th goal under Jürgen was scored by Darwin Nunez in the 5-1 Europa League victory at Sparta Prague in March 2024.

With the defeat of LASK earlier in 2023/24, Jürgen Klopp became the first Liverpool manager to reach the landmark of 50 wins in European football. He did so in 82 games. He surpassed the 49 won by Rafa Benitez.

Jürgen has taken charge of the club in more European games than any other manager. The ties against Atalanta BC saw Klopp reach 91 matches in European competition.

Two of Liverpool's three best seasons for goalscoring have come under the former Mainz and Borussia Dortmund coach. They scored 135 in 2017/18 before setting a new club record in 2021/22, netting 147 times. That total could be broken this season – currently 127 scored.

Jürgen's first signing was Marko Grujic, signed from Red Star Belgrade for £5.1 million in January 2016. His final acquisition was Bayern Munich's Ryan Gravenberch in September 2023 for a fee of £34.2 million.

He lost one of 18 Merseyside derby encounters – and nobody was there to watch it. The 2-0 defeat at an empty Anfield came in the Covid season of 2020/21.

Jürgen Klopp never lost a game as Liverpool manager on the opening day of the league season, winning five and drawing three.

He never lost on Boxing Day, recording victories in all six games. So far, he has never lost on the final day of a league campaign, winning six times and drawing twice.

The Reds under Jürgen Klopp have scored more league goals (45) against Arsenal than they have against any other team. Bournemouth and Crystal Palace are next on the list with 42 and 41 respectively.

The team Jürgen has won most league games against as Reds boss is Crystal Palace. He has defeated the Eagles 13 times, one more than West Ham.

In 32 League Cup matches as Reds boss he used 98 different players, while his final appearance at Wembley as Reds boss saw his team lift the Carabao Cup defeating Chelsea 1-0 thanks to Virgil van Dijk's 118th-minute winner.

Stats correct up to and including 14.04.24